LINDSTROM'S SUMMARY OF

EMPLOYMENT LAW

SECOND EDITION

Eric E. Johnson

LINDSTROM'S SUMMARIES OF THE LAW SERIES

THE JUNE COMPANY PRESS

To my father,
Ted Johnson,
who worked so that
others could work

Lindstrom's Summary of Employment Law, Second Edition

Lindstrom's Summary of the Law Series
A June Company Press Book

ISBN: 0-9705825-0-1

"The June Company," "The June Company Press," "Lindstrom's" and "Lindstrom's Summaries of the Law" are trademarks of The June Company.

http://www.juneco.net

DISCLAIMER:

This book is not designed for, nor should it be used by, persons seeking legal advice. The characterization of the law contained in this book may not apply to such persons. This is true in part because laws differ greatly from state to state and can change over time. Additionally, this book skips some details that might be important to a real case. Persons with legal problems regarding their employment should seek the counsel of a qualified attorney in their state or district.

TABLE OF CONTENTS

LIST OF ABBREVIATIONS

ADA	Americans with Disabilities Act of 1990
ADEA	Age Discrimination in Employment Act of 1967
BFOQ	Bona-fide occupational qualification
COBRA	In employment-law usage, refers to that portion of the Consolidated Omnibus Budget Reconciliation Act of 1985 which amended ERISA §§ 601–607 (29 U.S.C. §§ 1161–1167) so as to allow employees to continue employer-provided health insurance after termination of employment
DOL	Department of Labor
EEOC	Equal Employment Opportunity Commission
EPA	Equal Pay Act of 1963
ERISA	Employee Retirement Income Security Act of 1974
FLSA	Fair Labor Standards Act of 1938
FMLA	Family and Medical Leave Act of 1997
FUTA	Federal Unemployment Tax Act
HIPAA	Health Insurance Portability and Accountability Act of 1996
IIED	Intentional infliction of emotional distress
IRS	Internal Revenue Service
MHPA	Mental Health Parity Act of 1996
N.B.	Note well (from the Latin *noto bene*)
NLRA	National Labor Relations Act
NLRB	National Labor Relations Board
OSHA	Occupational Safety and Health Act *or* Occupational Safety and Health Administration
OSHRC	Occupational Safety and Health Review Commission
OWBPA	Older Workers Benefit Protection Act of 1990
PBGC	Pension Benefit Guaranty Corporation
Title VII	Title VII of the Civil Rights Act of 1964
Section 1981	The federal civil rights statute at 42 U.S.C. § 1981
Section 1983	The federal civil rights statute at 42 U.S.C. § 1983
WDVPP	Wrongful discharge in violation of public policy
U.S.	When used with a year in a case cite, refers to the United States Supreme Court
U.S.C.	United States Code
§ 1981	The federal civil rights statute at 42 U.S.C. § 1981
§ 1983	The federal civil rights statute at 42 U.S.C. § 1983

PREFACE

HOW TO USE STUDY GUIDES

While study guides are often effectively used as exam preparation at the end of the semester, a more valuable way to use this and other study guides is to read them and think about them early on in the course, or even before the course begins. Think of study guides not just as exam preparation, but as *course preparation*.

Armed with a framework of knowledge about a particular field of law as a whole—and many of its blackletter details—you can then use lectures and assigned cases to fill out that understanding. Study-guide preparation at the outset means you are less likely to be confused in class. You may also find that reading the study guide first makes your casebook reading faster and less frustrating: Instead of devoting your energy to picking out the nuggets of blackletter in an ocean of judicial prose, you can concentrate on evaluating the judge's spin on the issues and critique his or her arguments at a higher analytical level.

Ultimately, it is this higher analytical thinking that is going to be most valued by your professor. Study guides cannot give you this ability directly, but by aiding your understanding of the blackletter law, study guides can help free up your time and mental energy for the more rewarding tasks of critical analysis about the law and its policy aims.

Another, more pragmatic reason to read and work with the study guide earlier in the semester rather than later is that your professor's understanding of the law may differ from the content of this, or any other, study guide. This is true in part because reasonable scholars disagree about how to characterize the law. Any division of the law into discrete parts is a subjective exercise: Where one professor sees a three-prong test for a rule of substantive law, another professor might see a two-prong test for a rule of procedure. On the exam, you want to show mastery of your professor's view of the law—not the study-guide author's.

Of course, at the end of the semester, this study guide will serve as a reference as you prepare for the exam. If you have worked with it in the beginning of the semester, however, you will get more out of it as exam preparation, both because repetition aids recall and because you will have developed an understanding of how this book relates to your particular course.

ABOUT THIS STUDY GUIDE

While you will find that this study guide is like many others you may have seen, you may also notice that there are differences. For instance, this book specifically aims to clear up misunderstandings and frustrations that are introduced by the leading casebooks. You may also notice that this Lindstrom's Summary occasionally introduces relevant theory concepts. We have introduced this feature because of the increasing amount of classroom time being spent on academic criticism of the law.

This study guide was also designed with the realization that precious few students actually read the massive commercial outlines on the market. When using one of these outlines, students often rely on the "capsule summary"—often only a tenth of the book. Instead of carrying two outlines—one huge and the other very small—the outline in this Lindstrom's Summary seeks to strike a sensible balance. In editing, we have striven to make the outline manageable and readable, yet comprehensive. Instead of including an example for absolutely every concept, we have included examples only where we believed a student might be confused by a statement of blackletter law alone. And, wherever possible, we have eschewed hypotheticals for real cases from employment-law casebooks.

GIVE US YOUR FEEDBACK

While we believe our editorial philosophy is on target, putting that philosophy into practice requires your feedback. Do we have too much detail in one place? Not enough in another? What concepts or doctrines did your class cover that this Lindstrom's Summary did not?

As a reader of the Second Edition, you have gained the benefit of the wisdom of many students who have told us how to improve. We paid careful attention to all comments, and this book is different because of them. We invite you to make a similar impact on the Third Edition. Please send your comments, including general feedback and notice of any errors to eejohnso@email.com.

ACKNOWLEDGEMENTS

Very special thanks for the editorial assistance of Kit Augustson, J.D. Boalt Hall '00. Thanks also to everyone who provided feedback and advice on the First Edition.

— E.E.J.

CHAPTER I

WHO IS AN EMPLOYEE?

A. Introduction

A person who works for another is not necessarily an "employee." Persons who are not employees, but who work for another person or firm, usually fall into the category of "independent contractors." The status of "employee" brings to bear a special set of rights and duties under the law that does not apply when the person merely contracts to do work for another.

The same person might be classified as an employee under one statute or legal doctrine but not under a different one. For instance, a person might qualify as an employee under the Fair Labor Standards Act, but not under the Internal Revenue Code. Additionally, some regulatory statutes may cover persons even if they are not "employees."

Circumstances determine whether or not it is in the interest of workers or firms to characterize their relationship as an employee-employer relationship. Would-be employers and employees often have differing interests, and therefore contest the classification.

B. Employees vs. Independent Contractors

1. **Disadvantages and Advantages of the Employee Classification**—Classifying workers as "independent contractors" rather than "employees" can create substantial advantages for a firm. With the "independent contractor" classification, would-be employers may be able to avoid provisions of the Fair Labor Standards Act (FLSA) including minimum wage and overtime pay. Independent-contractor status can also excuse firms from paying Social Security taxes and unemployment-insurance premiums on behalf of their workers. One advantage for employers in having workers classified as "employees" is that worker's compensation laws can be used to preclude tort suits by injured workers.

2. **"Right-to-Control" Common-Law Test**—Under the common law, a worker is an employee if the employer can control the manner in which the work is done. In contrast, **a worker is an independent contractor if the hiring party controls only the ultimate result** of the work, leaving decisions about when and how to do the work to the contractor.

   a. *Example:* A software programmer is hired to create a spell-checker for a word-processing program. The firm sets the parameters of the needed programming, occasionally meets with the programmer to resolve technical problems, and takes delivery of the programming. This programmer would be an independent contractor. However, if the programmer were hired into a department where the company supervised his work and directed his tasks to fit into the effort of the whole programming team, the programmer would be an employee.

b. Note that **the right-to-control test is *narrower* than the economic realities test**, discussed *infra*. That is, the right-to-control test classifies fewer people as employees.

c. **The IRS uses the common-law test** to determine whether workers are employees for the purposes of federal taxation. The IRS adds to or modifies the test, however, by setting out a list of factors to assist in determining which employees fall under the common-law definition.

3. **The Economic-Realities Test**—Under the Fair Labor Standards Act (FLSA), whether someone is an employee depends on the "economic reality" of the relationship, as opposed to the common-law focus on formalistic issues of control over work. The economic-realities test is, under the totality of the circumstances, **if the worker is economically dependent on the hiring party, then the worker is an employee**. *Secretary of Labor v. Lauritzen* (7th Cir. 1988) and *Donovan v. DialAmerica Marketing, Inc.* (3d Cir. 1985) use six factors for the economic-realities test.

a. *Control*—If a defendant controls the manner in which the work is done, rather then relinquishing control to the worker, the defendant is an employer.

   i. Note that this one factor is similar to the entire common-law test.

b. *Profit and Loss*—The more exposure workers have to profit and loss, the less likely they are to be employees. Contractors face a risk of loss and the possibility of achieving higher profits through the better management of their work.

c. *Capital Investment*—Interrelated to profit-and-loss, the more of an investment workers make in tools, supplies, or other initial outlays, the less likely they are to be employees.

d. *Degree of Skill Required*—A high degree of skill militates in favor of workers not being employees.

e. *Permanency*—The more temporary the relationship, the less likely it is to be an employment relationship. Permanent arrangements (even if they are seasonal and recurring) favor finding that workers are employees.

f. *Integral Part of Hiring Party's Business*—The more integral the work is to the would-be employer's business the more likely it is that the persons doing such work are employees.

   i. *Example:* Special efficiency consultants hired to streamline an automobile manufacturing process would be independent contractors. Assembly-line workers, however, who are employees, are integral to the core business of an automobile manufacturer.

g. **Dependence of Workers**—The more the workers depend upon income from the defendant, the more likely it is that they are employees. Independent contractors often have more than one party for which they work.

4. **Statutory Function Test**—In a concurrence to *Lauritzen*, Judge Easterbrook advocated looking at the intended function of the statute at issue to determine whether workers should be treated as employees.

5. **Ability to Contract Out of Employee Status**—Most statutes prevent workers and firms from contracting out of the employment relationship. Courts will look to the circumstances of the relationship, regardless of what label the parties have agreed to.

   a. **The Vizcaino Case:** Microsoft hired workers as "independent contractors," but the workers were determined to have the legal status of employees. These employees were entitled to retroactively awarded employee benefits, even though they had contracted for compensation without such benefits. *Vizcaino v. Microsoft Corp.* (9th Cir. 1997).

C. Coverage of Statutes

1. **Specific Statutory Definitions of Employees**—Statutes utilize different definitions of "employee." The definitions may be contained in the language of the act, or developed through caselaw.

   See discussion of individual statutes to determine whether a worker would be considered an employee for that specific law.

2. **Covered Employers and Employees**—Statutes may exempt employers and employees from their provisions for various reasons. For instance, federal and state statutes usually limit their coverage to firms with a certain minimum number of employees. Federal statutes also are generally limited to firms or industries that have a connection to interstate commerce.

   See discussion of individual statutes in this outline to determine coverage under those laws.

CHAPTER II

DISCHARGE

N.B.: Following the pattern of casebooks and classroom instructors, this chapter includes law that is applicable to more than discharge. For instance, demotion, reduction in pay, or disciplinary action may be actionable as a breach of employment contract or a tortious wrongful discharge regardless of whether the employee is fired or forced to quit.

A. The At-Will Rule

1. **Definition**—An employment relationship is presumed to be "at will," absent a contract to the contrary. "At will" means that the employer may discharge the employee **for any reason or for no reason at all, at any time and without notice**. The employee has the complementary right to quit at any time and for any reason.

2. **Majority Rule**—The at-will rule is the law of the majority of jurisdictions.

3. **Function**—In most jurisdictions, the at-will rule functions procedurally as a presumption of at-will status between the employer and employee. This presumption is overcome when a discharged employee shows a valid agreement with the employer that provides for some other standard of discharge.

    a. A minority of states view the at-will rule as a substantive rule of contracts.

4. **Pretextual Reasons for Firing an At-Will Employee**—If the employee is fired for reasons that are shown to be false, some courts hold that the employee must be given a chance to rebut the charges before being discharged. *Prout v. Sears, Roebuck & Co.* (Mont. 1989).

5. **Exceptions, Limitations, Modifications, and Repudiations of the At-Will Rule**— Many doctrines make the at-will rule inapplicable in certain situations and jurisdictions. These doctrines, described *infra* at II.C–G, along with the underlying at-will rule, make up the common law of discharge. Various statutory schemes have modified this body of law.

B. Constructive Discharge

To have a cause of action for discharge, the employee usually must be fired. Generally, if the employee voluntarily quits, then there can be no cause of action for discharge. The doctrine of "constructive discharge," however, sometimes allows employees who have quit to sue as if they had been discharged. The focus is on whether the quit was truly "voluntary."

1. **Intolerable Working Conditions**—If the employer creates conditions that would cause any reasonable employee to quit, there is a constructive discharge.

a. ***Minority Requirement: Intent***—Some jurisdictions require the plaintiff/employee to prove that the defendant/employer created the intolerable conditions with the intent of making the employee quit.

2. **Employer Breach of Contract**—If the employer breaches the contract by demoting, reassigning or reducing the pay or responsibilities of an employee, the breach can constitute constructive discharge if those conditions were part of an employment contract.

3. **Not Receiving Pay**—An employer's withholding of wages or salary rightfully due the employee can constitute constructive discharge.

4. **Duress and Threatening Conduct by the Employer**—Where the employer threatens that the employee must resign or face termination, threatens to give poor references to future prospective employers, and/or threatens other maleficent consequences, the termination is generally considered to be involuntary.

C. Standards for Discharge

The following standards for discharge can become relevant either because a contract between the employer and employee has specified a particular standard for termination or because a certain standard is applied through the operation of statute or the common law.

> *Beware: While the various standards for discharge discussed in this section are theoretically distinguishable, courts sometimes use the terms—and the concepts behind them—interchangeably.*

1. **The At-Will Standard**—The most common "standard" for discharge is at-will. At-will employment, however, might be better thought of as the *absence* of a standard, since it means that either party may terminate the employment relationship for any reason at any time. The standards discussed immediately below restrict employers from some discharges that would be otherwise allowable in an at-will relationship.

2. **The Just Cause Standard**—The just-cause standard requires that the employer have "just cause" to terminate the employee. The same standard is sometimes referred to as "good cause" or simply "cause."

a. ***When Applicable***—The just-cause standard **usually comes into play when a contract prescribes a definite term for the employment**. The just-cause standard is also applicable whenever a contract expressly enumerates a just-cause standard, whether the contract is for a definite or indefinite term. Union contracts that are the result of a collective-bargaining agreement often include a provision for a just-cause standard. Nonunion contracts may also specify a just-cause standard, although such provisions are rare. The just-cause standard is also used in some tort contexts (discussed *infra* at II.F). In Montana, where the at-will rule has been revoked, a statute specifies a just-cause standard for employment beyond a probationary period. Just cause is also the standard for public-employees (discussed *infra* at II.J).

b. ***What Constitutes Just Cause***—Two broad categories describe just cause for firing an employee:

    i.   ***Employee performance***—If an employee fails to perform his job adequately or commits serious or willful misconduct, the employer will generally have just cause to discharge the employee.

        1)   ***Substantiality requirement***—The misconduct or failure to perform must be substantial. That is, occasional excusable absences, slight neglectfulness, or even transient rudeness will not give rise to just cause for termination.

        2)   ***Off-work behavior usually exempted***—Courts will often refuse to find just cause for conduct that takes place outside the workplace. For instance, drinking during off-hours may not be just cause.

    ii.   ***Employer circumstances***—Jurisdictions are split as to whether adverse economic conditions, bona-fide plant closings, or management reorganization may constitute just cause.

        1)   The allowance for business circumstances usually will not qualify as just cause if there is an employment contract for a definite term, even if such circumstances are generally considered just cause in the jurisdiction.

c. ***Compared to Good Faith***—Just cause is an objective standard. That is, application of the common law determines what grounds constitute just cause for termination, rather than the facts of the particular case. This stands in contrast to the subjective good-faith standard.

3. The Good-Faith Standard—Good faith is a subjective standard, revolving around the intent of the employer. That is, whether or not a discharge was in good faith depends on the employer's subjective state-of-mind in firing the employee. The good-faith standard is primarily used in the contractual doctrine of the implied covenant of good faith and fair dealing (discussed *infra* at II.E.2).

4. The Satisfactory-Performance Standard—A contract for "satisfactory performance" sets a very low standard for discharge. The satisfactory-performance standard allows discharge whenever an employer does not find the employee's performance satisfactory. Generally, an employee can show wrongful discharge under this standard if she can prove that the employer was not, in fact, dissatisfied by her performance.

a. ***Status Vis-a-Vis At-Will***—Some courts hold that a contract for satisfactory performance results in a standard indistinguishable from the at-will rule. *Gordon v. Matthew-Bender* (N.D. Ill. 1983).

b. ***Can Imply Other Standards***—Some courts may find a contract for satisfactory performance to imply a just-cause or good-faith basis for termination. *Hetes v. Schefman & Miller Law Office* (Mich. App. 1986).

5. **Other Standards**—As a matter of contract, the parties to an employment relationship can set any standard they wish. The above standards tend to be used by courts to interpret contracts that do not explicitly set more specific standards. Carefully negotiated contracts with executives or other high-level employees may set complex substantive and procedural requirements for termination. Collective bargaining agreements with union employees often contain more detailed statements on the standards for termination.

D. Contracting Out of At-Will

The at-will rule is only a presumption or default rule in lieu of a contract to the contrary. If the employer and employee agree to another standard for termination, the at-will presumption is not an issue.

> **FOR BETTER UNDERSTANDING:** Casebooks and professors sometimes characterize "contracting out" as an "exception" to or even an "erosion" of the at-will rule. The at-will rule itself, however, is self-limiting to situations where there is no agreement to the contrary. Therefore, most contractual agreements that set a higher standard for termination (whether express or implied-in-fact) are not really modifications to the at-will rule at all—the rule is simply inapplicable to such situations. Note that implied-in-law contracts (discussed *infra* at II.D.2), however, represent an actual departure from the at-will rule, since their existence *in law*— and not *in fact*—means that there is something in the law beyond an unmodified at-will rule.

> Of course, even where judges make decisions "on the facts," the more liberally they construe those facts to the benefit of the employee, the more one could say that they are modifying the at-will rule.

1. **Express Contracts**—Express contracts are those that clearly and directly spell out a binding agreement between two parties, and they may be either written or oral. Express contracts are distinguished from "implied contracts."

   a. *Written Contracts*—When the parties create a written agreement to set the terms and conditions of employment, the court will generally uphold that agreement.

      i. *Requirement of consideration*—As is true generally under contract law, there must be consideration to support the finding of a valid contract. While this can often be a point of contention with regard to oral contracts and employment manuals (discussed *infra* at II.D.1.b–c), it is generally not an issue with express written contracts.

      ii. *Fixed (or definite) term of employment*—A contract for a definite term of employment will imply, in absence of an express provision to the contrary, that the employee cannot be fired except for just cause during the term. *Chiodo v. General Waterworks Corp.* (Utah 1966).

         1) *The rate-of-pay rule*—The rate-of-pay rule holds that if a contract sets a salary or wage stated as a certain amount of money per unit

of time, then **the contract will last for at least that period of time**. So if a salary is stated in "per month" or "per year" terms, then the contract will be read to be for a definite term of at least one month or one year, respectively. Jurisdictions are split on the validity of the rate-of-pay rule. See, e.g., *Bernard v. IMI Systems* (N.J. 1993) (an $80,000-per-year salary did not establish a minimum one-year duration).

2) *Notice provisions*—A contract that provides for a period of notice before a party may terminate employment, such as 15-days notice, usually **sets a fixed term of employment for the notice period**.

3) *Probationary periods*—Courts are split on whether continuing to be employed beyond a probationary period implies a higher standard for discharge than at-will. Where a probationary period means that the employee can be fired at any time for any reason, some courts have held that the expiration of such a period implies that there is some higher standard afterward. The majority, however, hold that a probationary period is consistent with subsequent at-will employment.

4) *The just-cause defense*—Proving that an employee was fired for just cause constitutes a defense for the employer.

5) *Definite term / remedies for employer*—If an employee quits or commits a material breach of the employment contract during the term of the contract, the employee is liable for the difference between the employee's wage and the wage required to hire a replacement for the remainder of the term, if the replacement wage is higher. The employee may also be liable for foreseeable consequential damages.

   a) *No specific performance*—The employer generally cannot obtain the remedy of specific performance. Courts cannot force the employee to work for the remainder of the term; such a court order would violate the 13th Amendment's prohibition of involuntary servitude.

      i) *Negative* specific performance, i.e., enjoining the employee from working elsewhere, may be enforceable. (See III.B and C.)

   b) *Rarely sought*—Cases where employers actually sought and received damages from breaching employees are very rare.

6) *Definite term / remedies for employee*—If the employer terminates the employee before the end of the term, or otherwise commits a material breach of the contract, the employee may recover lost wages, but has **a duty to mitigate** by looking for **similar employment in the same locale**. The wages from the new

job will be deducted from the amount owed to the employee by the old employer.

- a) ***Damages in lieu of mitigation***—If the employee fails to attempt to mitigate damages by looking for similar work in the same locale, then the employer may deduct from the recovery the wages the employee *would have* received from such employment.

- b) ***No subsequent similar employment***—If no such mitigating employment can be found through the employee's reasonable efforts, then no deduction will be made from the damages due the employee.

- c) ***Non-similar employment***—If the employee does not find similar work within the same locale, then the employee has no duty to accept non-similar employment. However, if an employee accepts any employment—regardless of how similar it is—those wages will be deducted from the employee's recovery against the previous employer.

7) ***Statutory right to terminate***—Some jurisdictions have created a statutory right to terminate. The statutory right allows employers to terminate employees in cases of habitual neglect or continued incapacity *despite* contractual provisions for a fixed term.

b. ***Employment Manuals as Written Contracts***

i. ***Generally enforceable***—Where an employment manual (or "handbook") is distributed to employees and contains clear and specific provisions regarding job security, a majority of jurisdictions will enforce the manual in contract. Because the distribution of a manual does not fit into the ordinary scenario of the creation of a bilateral contract through mutual consideration, courts have used different theories to make manuals enforceable.

1) ***As unilateral contracts***—Most courts rely on a theory of unilateral contract to enforce handbook promises. The doctrine of unilateral contracts **allows enforcement even where there is no mutuality of obligation or additional consideration**. So, a manual distributed after hiring has the same effect as if presented before.

2) ***Through promissory estoppel***—Some courts enforce employment manuals under a theory of promissory estoppel. Where an employee reasonably and detrimentally relies upon the employer's promise in the manual, then the court will enforce the promise if doing so is necessary to avoid injustice. (Promissory estoppel discussed in detail *infra* at II.E.1.)

3) ***Minority view: Not enforceable***—A minority of jurisdictions refuse to enforce employment manuals **on the basis that there is**

no consideration. Since the employee's work is consideration for his wages, these courts hold that there needs to be additional consideration from the worker to bind the employer to promises of enhanced job security. Even under this minority rule, however, employment-manual promises may be enforced if there is clear additional consideration. For example, if, based on the promise in the manual, the employee rejected other, lucrative job offers, a court might enforce the promise.

ii. ***Rescinding the manual***—Courts that enforce manuals are split on whether an employer may modify or rescind promises of job security after making the original promise. Under ordinary contract law, of course, one party may not unilaterally rescind a contract and thereby end their obligation to perform.

    1) ***One view: Terminable if the employer provides reasonable notice***—Some jurisdictions hold that employers can change job-security provisions if they provide reasonable notice. These courts reason that when the employer distributes a revised manual, it provides an offer for a modified contract. By coming to work the next day, these courts reason, the employee signals acceptance of the offer. *Bankey v. Storer Broadcasting* (Mich. 1989) (promises in an employee manual can be revoked with reasonable notice).

    2) ***Alternate view: Lack of consideration prevents employees from being bound***—Other courts hold that an offer for a modified contract rescinding job security cannot bind the employee, because the employee gains no benefit that constitutes consideration. Under this view, continued payment of wages is not a benefit gained, and therefore is not consideration.

iii. ***Disclaimers***—Employers may defend against claims based on employment manuals by pointing to a disclaimer in the manual stating that the employment relationship is terminable at-will.

    1) ***Prominence of disclaimer***—Courts are split on how prominent the disclaimer must be in order to vitiate the effect of promises within the remainder of the handbook. Some courts hold that the disclaimer must be prominently displayed or conspicuous to dispel the effect of job-security promises. Other courts hold that as long as the manual includes a disclaimer, there is no requirement of prominence.

c. ***Oral Contracts***—Oral contracts are generally enforceable in the same manner as written contracts. There are, however, some special problems associated with oral contracts.

i. ***Casual words of encouragement***—Remarks characterized as mere causal words of encouragement do not function to create a contract. For example, an employer saying that a job is a good one in which to "stay and grow" did not function as a binding promise of job security. *Forman v. BRI Corp.* (E.D. Pa. 1982).

ii. ***"Lifetime" or "permanent" employment***—Courts differ widely on the interpretation of oral promises for "lifetime" or "permanent" employment. The moderate position views the resulting contract as setting a just-cause standard for discharge. At the extremes, courts view the resulting contract to require the employer to provide employment until the employee dies or quits; alternatively, some courts view the relationship as nothing more than at-will.

iii. ***Requirement of consideration***—Consideration, which is less important in the context of express written contracts, assumes a greater importance in litigation about oral contracts. "Additional" or "independent" consideration—beyond merely coming to work the next day—militates in favor of the employee because it is evidence of the validity of the contract. For example, if an employee leaves a stable job because of another employer's oral promise of job security, courts may consider such action or forbearance to constitute independent consideration.

> ***FOR BETTER UNDERSTANDING:*** The use of consideration doctrine in this manner can be confusing to the student. While courts speak of substantive contract law, they appear instead to make an evidentiary determination of whether a binding contract has been formed. No matter how the courts word their opinions, however, there is a notable reluctance to rearrange legal rights between parties when their words of agreement seem to be somewhat frivolous. Stricter requirements—through either evidence law or contract law—help allay the courts' concerns about whether a contract actually existed.

iv. ***Statute of frauds***—A principle of general contract law, the statute of frauds **voids all oral contracts that cannot be completely performed within one year**. The interpretation of this rule becomes problematic when applied to a promise of employment with just-cause-only termination where the agreement is not subject to a definite term of less than a year.

   1) ***Enforceable where the term is defined without reference to time***—If the contract provides that full performance will occur upon the happening of some future event, without reference to time, then the contract is enforceable.

      a) ***Lifetime contracts***—Because an employee could die within one year, a contract for lifetime employees does not violate the statute of frauds in a majority of jurisdictions.

b)   ***Example:*** A contract to work as a physical therapist until a certain patient recovers is enforceable, since the patient could theoretically recover within one year—even if such recovery were highly unlikely in reality.

2)   ***Unenforceable where the term is defined as longer than one year***—In virtually all jurisdictions, if the contract is for a definite term of more than a year, it will barred by the statute. For instance, if the oral contract guarantees employment until 2010, and the contract is made in 2005, then the statute will bar enforcement.

    a)   ***Notice provisions***—Provisions allowing for termination upon a period of notice of less than a year do not save an oral contract from being voided under the statute of frauds according to the majority view.

        i)   ***Example:*** An oral contract for two years of employment provides that it is terminable upon two weeks notice. The enforcement of the contract is barred by the statute of frauds, because it is not capable of full performance within a year.

        ii)   ***Minority view:*** According the minority view, a provision allowing for non-breaching termination within a year takes the contract out of the statute of frauds. The *Restatement (Second) of Contracts* is in accord with this minority view.

    b)   ***Time of contracting and completion control***—The time relevant for the statute of frauds is not technically the duration of employment, but the time from contracting to completion. So, where the date of completion is a year or more from the time of contracting, the contract is unenforceable because of the statute of frauds.

        i)   ***Example:*** In January of 2000, a person agrees to be employed for four hours as a bartender at a wedding in June 2001. Although the duration of employment is for less than a year, the date of completion is more than a year from the date of contracting, so the agreement is unenforceable.

3)   ***Minority view: Indefinite duration contracts within statute of frauds***—A minority of jurisdictions hold that the statute of frauds will bar enforcement of oral promises of job security without a fixed term. This includes an oral promise not to fire an employee except for just cause. These courts rely on the theory that the statute of frauds only allows enforcement of oral contracts capable of *non-breaching performance* within one year. These courts reason that firing an employee is not performance but, instead, is excuse of the employer's performance because of the employee's breach.

4)   *Application of promissory estoppel*—Even where the statute of frauds bars enforcement of the contract, courts **may still enforce the promise by using the doctrine of promissory estoppel** (*infra* at II.E.1).

v.   *Parol evidence rule*—A general doctrine applicable to contracts, the parol evidence rule prohibits the introduction of outside evidence to vary or contradict the terms of a written contract that is intended to be the parties' final and complete expression of their agreement. Employers can use the parol evidence rule where employees allege oral promises of job security and where the employer subsequently obtained a written contract for at-will employment.

1)   The parol evidence rule has many exceptions or circumstances in which it is inapplicable, including:

a)   Evidence of a later oral modification or new oral contract is not barred by the rule, because the evidence is not being used to contradict the written document; instead, it is being used as evidence of a *new* bargain.

b)   Oral statements made at the time of signing the contract can be admitted as evidence to aid in the *interpretation* of the contract but not in contradicting its terms.

2. **Implied-in-Fact Contracts**—Unlike express written or oral contracts, implied-in-fact contracts are not accompanied by any communication that directly expresses a bargain between the parties. Instead, courts may find that a contract exists by virtue of the circumstances of the relationship. Courts may look at factors such as independent consideration, the employer's personnel policies or practices, the employee's longevity of service, actions or communications by the employer reflecting assurances, or industry-wide practices. *Pugh v. See's Candies* (Cal. App. 1981).

a.   *Compared with Implied-in-Law Contracts*—An implied-in-fact contract is considered an actual contract—a bargain arrived at through a meeting of the minds—even though there are no express words of agreement. An implied-in-law contract, however, is not really a contract at all, but a legal construction in which the court, for the sake of fairness, will award damages as if there were a contract.

b.   In some jurisdictions, all contract claims that are not based on individual express written contracts are litigated under the doctrine of implied-in-fact contracts. These include employment handbooks and oral representations (*supra* at II.D.1.b–c).

c.   *Standard for Discharge*—While implied-in-fact contracts could include various standards for discharge, courts commonly find a just-cause standard in these agreements.

d.   *The* **Pugh** *Case*—Over 32 years, Wayne Pugh worked his way up from dishwasher to vice president in charge of production and member of the board of directors of See's Candies. Fired without explanation, Pugh argued that he was fired for stating he would refuse to take part in illegal dealings with a union. The court held that based on length-of-service and other circumstances of the relationship, a jury could have found that there was a valid implied-in-fact agreement that set a higher standard for discharge, such as just cause. *Pugh v. See's Candies* (Cal. App. 1981).

e. ***Theory Note***—Notice that "good" employers—those who have a tradition of treating employees fairly and not firing them capriciously—are the ones who bear the brunt of the implied-in-fact contract doctrine. Employers who cause employees to feel as if they are under constant threat of being fired would almost certainly be victorious in an implied-in-fact-contract claim because the circumstances would indicate a lack of any implied promise of job security.

E. Implied-in-Law Contractual Exceptions to At-Will

Implied-in-law contracts are not "contracts" in the real sense. Instead, courts award damages *as if* there were a contract between the parties, because not doing so would be unjust. As discussed above, actual contracts, whether express or implied-in-fact, are not "exceptions" to the at-will rule, because the at-will rule is only a default rule, and parties are free to contract around it. Implied-in-law contracts, however, are properly characterized as legal exceptions to the at-will doctrine in those jurisdictions where they are recognized.

1. **Promissory Estoppel / Reliance Doctrine**—When an element necessary for the formation of a contract is missing, such as consideration, the courts may enforce the promise nevertheless with the doctrine of *promissory estoppel*. The doctrine applies when the employee **relied on the employer's promise to the employee's detriment** and **such reliance was reasonable**.

   a. ***Section 90***—The Restatement (Second) of Contracts *§ 90* is the definitive modern formulation of reliance doctrine or promissory estoppel: "A promise which the promisor should reasonably expect to induce action or forbearance on the part of the promisee or a third person and which does induce such action or forbearance is binding if injustice can be avoided only by enforcement of the promise…"

   b. ***Is Reliance Consideration?*** Authorities and scholars differ on whether reliance allows enforcement of the contract in the absence of consideration or whether the reliance itself is a form of consideration creating an actual contract. The more widely held view is the former, but under either theory, the result is the same.

   c. ***The Detriment Requirement***—Quitting a job in reliance on another job offer will usually constitute a detriment for purposes of promissory estoppel. Lesser detriments, such as passing up other job offers, or passing up the opportunity to look for other job offers, are less likely to meet the requirement. Some courts refer to the requirement of a "special detriment." See, e.g., *Veno v. Meredith* (Pa. 1986).

d. ***The Reasonableness Requirement***—The most contestable aspect of promissory estoppel claims is whether the reliance was reasonable. For example, one court found that relocating a family from Argentina to California for an offer of at-will employment was not reasonable. *Ferrerya v. E&J Gallo Winery* (Cal. App. 1964).

e. ***The* Grouse *Case***—Grouse, a pharmacist, was offered a job at Group Health Plan. He resigned his current position in order to accept the GHP offer. After accepting the offer, but before starting employment, GHP informed Grouse that they had hired someone else and had no job for him. Because of the bilateral power of termination, no contract existed in fact, but § 90 of the *Restatement (Second) of Contracts* allowed the finding of an implied-in-law contract; GHP knew that Grouse would resign in reliance upon the job offer and thus incur the detriment of not having the previous job. *Grouse v. Group Health Plan* (Minn. 1981).

f. ***Damages***—Ordinarily, damages under a promissory estoppel claim are *reliance damages*. That is, the damages equal the amount required to restore the plaintiff to the position he was in before he relied upon the promise and incurred the detriment. Compare this to traditional-contract-law *expectation damages*, which are those that would put the plaintiff into the position he would be in had the contract been completed.

2. **The Implied Covenant of Good Faith and Fair Dealing**—All contracts are generally considered to have an implied covenant of good faith and fair dealing. This covenant requires parties to carry out genuine and fair efforts to effectuate the intended bargain.

   a. ***Majority Approach: Not Generally Applicable to Employment Contracts***—Despite the covenant's status in general contract law, most courts have carved out an exception for employment contracts, thus insulating employers from claims that they have fired at-will employees in bad faith. Courts reason that applying the covenant to employment relationships would upset employer goals and contradict the at-will doctrine, which allows termination at any time and for any reason without limitation.

   b. ***First Minority Approach: Deprivation of the Benefit of the Bargain***—Some states apply the covenant in order to allow an employee to recover the benefit of an employment contract that the employee has fairly earned before termination.

      i. ***The* Fortune *Case***—A paid-by-commission 25-year employee was fired the day after taking a $5 million order. The court held that the termination was designed to deprive him of the $92,000 commission, and therefore was in bad faith. *Fortune v. National Cash Register* (Mass. 1977).

   c. ***Second Minority Approach: Covenant Generally Applicable***—Although rare, some courts have recognized a *general* good-faith-and-fair-dealing limitation on terminations. While not as limiting as a just-cause standard, the application of the covenant in this manner goes beyond the benefits analysis. It allows recovery for terminations in which like employees are treated in unlike ways and where public policy issues are implicated. (See II.F. for discussion of public policy aims in the context of tort actions.)

F. Tort Actions for Discharge

Unlike most claims based on contract doctrine, the tort claims relating to discharge cannot generally be "contracted around." That is, for wrongful discharge in violation of public policy and intentional infliction of emotional distress, it does not matter what contract an employee signs ahead of time; the employee may still sue.

1. **Wrongful Discharge in Violation of Public Policy (WDVPP)**—A majority of states recognize the tort of wrongful discharge in violation of public policy, also called "the public policy tort." Unlike traditional torts, which seek to compensate a victim because of injury to that victim, WDVPP claims may only be brought when there is a strong connection between the discharge and harm to the public at large—not just to the employee-plaintiff. The discharge is tortious in this way if some clearly stated societal or public need is directly frustrated. The archetypal example is discharge for jury duty. Allowing employees to be fired for serving on a jury would undermine the jury system and would therefore be an injury to the public.

   a. *Categories of Public Policy*—The following are the four most common categories of public policies that invoke WDVPP. States differ, however, in which categories and specific policies they recognize for tortious wrongful discharge.

      i. *Refusing to violate the law*—If an employee is ordered to violate the law and is then fired for refusing, the discharge will often be actionable as WDVPP. Standards differ, with most jurisdictions applying WDVPP for refusing to commit a crime, and a very few states applying WDVPP to discharge for refusing to commit a tort. *Petermann v. Teamsters* (Cal. App. 1959) (allowing a WDVPP claim for discharge where an employee refused to perjure testimony to legislature).

      ii. *Performing a public obligation*—Discharge for performing a public obligation or civic duty may be actionable under WDVPP. Such public obligations include jury service, obeying a subpoena, and testifying in court. *Nees v. Hocks* (Ore. 1975) (allowing a WDVPP claim for discharge where an employee served jury duty counter to the employer's wishes).

      iii. *Exercising a statutory right*—Where statutes provide affirmative rights to employees, many courts will treat discharge for exercising that right to be a tort, even if the statute does not contain a specific anti-retaliation provision. Courts commonly use this analysis for the exercise of rights under workers' compensation laws. *Frampton v. Central Indiana Gas* (Ind. 1973) (allowing a WDVPP claim for discharge where an employee filed a worker's compensation claim).

iv. ***Whistleblowing***—Many courts will protect employees from discharge "whistleblowing," i.e., reporting the illegal or dangerous activity of an employer.

    1) ***External whistleblowing***—External whistleblowing is reporting illegal or injurious conduct to someone outside the employer, such as the police or some other state agency. This external whistleblowing is the kind most often giving rise to a claim of action under WDVPP.

    2) ***Internal whistleblowing***—Internal whistleblowing is reporting wrongdoing to someone within the employer organization, such as a supervisor or review committee. Most jurisdictions provide less protection for such internal whistleblowers, dismissing the termination as a matter that does not involve the public-at-large in a direct enough manner to create a claim under WDVPP.

    3) ***Whistleblowing statutes***—Enacted in various jurisdictions, whistleblowing statutes, (discussed *infra* at II.G.), may or may not preclude a common-law tort claim for discharge incident to whistleblowing.

b. ***Finding a public policy***—Courts may look to various sources for identifying public policy that is to be protected by WDVPP. States differ, but statutes, constitutions, and court opinions are common places for finding public policy. Courts may also look to codified professional ethics, when, for instance, the employee is a nurse, accountant, or lawyer. States vary in their application of public policy, so even if a plaintiff can identify a public policy advanced by a statute or by a constitution, a court may still refuse to allow a WDVPP claim.

c. ***Remedies***—As contrasted with contract-doctrine claims, WDVPP is a tort, giving rise to tort damages, including punitive damages. Because of this, WDVPP awards can be much larger than contract-based actions.

2. **Intentional Infliction of Emotional Distress (IIED)**—When an employer knowingly or intentionally causes an employee severe mental anguish through extreme and outrageous conduct, that employee may have a cause of action for intentional infliction of emotional distress. Because IIED is an intentional tort, the right to sue for it cannot generally be waived by contract.

a. ***The* Wilson *Case***—A corporate vice president with 30 years of industry experience and a good track record was stripped of his duties and demoted to a warehouse position in which he spent most of his time performing janitorial tasks such as sweeping and cleaning up after other employees in the lunch area. After being exposed to constant humiliation, he was hospitalized for depression. His treatment included being locked in a padded cell and undergoing electric shock therapy. A judgment for $3.4 million against the employer for IIED was upheld on appeal. *Wilson v. Monarch Paper Co.* (5th Cir. 1991).

…aims may be preempted by workers' compensation laws in

…oyees may sometimes sue their employer under other torts such
…risonment, tortious interference with contract, defamation, or
…or retention.

…lower Statutes

…**tion**—Whistleblower laws protect employees from being retaliated against
… *…istleblowing*, i.e., reporting employer wrongdoing.

2. **Coverage of State Statutes**—A majority of states have whistleblower laws that
    protect public employees. A significant minority of states' whistleblower laws also
    protect private sector employees who report employer activities that are illegal or
    hazardous to the public.

    a. Whistleblower statutes generally do not protect employees for reporting breaches
        of company policy or for other misbehavior that is not illegal or dangerous to the
        public.

3. **Coverage of Federal Statutes**

    a. *Statutes for Federal Employees*—The Civil Service Reform Act and the
        Whistleblower Protection Act protect federal-employee whistleblowers.

    b. *Anti-retaliation Provisions of Other Statutes*—Many federal statutes, such as
        anti-discrimination statutes, contain anti-retaliation provisions that protect all
        covered private and public sector employees who make complaints under the
        statute.

    c. *Federal False Claims Act of 1863*—Amended in 1986, this Civil War statute
        encourages whistleblowing among the employees of government contractors.
        Contractors who defraud the federal government are liable for treble damages,
        and the whistleblower is allowed between 15 to 25 percent of the recovery as a
        financial incentive. (One executive for a military helicopter contractor was
        personally awarded $22.5 million under the act.)

4. **Good-Faith Basis**—Generally, whistleblowers must have a good-faith basis for
    believing that the alleged wrongdoing is actually taking place, but in order to have a
    claim under the whistleblower statute it usually not necessary for the alleged
    wrongdoing to be proven.

5. **External vs. Internal Reporting**—Commonly, whistleblower statutes only protect
    an employee's reporting wrongdoing to outside authorities, not to supervisors or
    review committees within the employer company. State statutes may, however,
    require an employee to report internally before reporting externally.

6. **Tort of Wrongful Discharge for Violation of Public Policy**—The common-law
    action of WDVPP may also be used to vindicate a whistleblower and may or may not
    be precluded by a whistleblower statute. (See *supra* at II.F.1.)

H. WARN

1. **The Worker Adjustment and Retraining Notification Act of 1988** requires employers with more than 100 employees to give workers 60 days advanced notice of mass layoffs or plant closings.

2. **Definition of "Mass Layoff"**—A "mass layoff" is defined as the dismissal of 500 employees, or a dismissal that encompasses a minimum of 33-percent of the full-time workforce and 50 full-time employees.

3. **Recovery**—WARN provides for a private right of action for damages of backpay for 60 days, attorneys' fees, and a $500 civil penalty per day.

I. Public Employees

Public employees receive significantly greater protection against discharge than private-sector employees do. There are both statutory and constitutional bases for this protection.

1. **Statutory Protections**

   a. **The Lloyd-LaFollete Act of 1912** prohibits dismissal of a member of the civil service unless it promotes the "efficiency of the service."

   b. **The Civil Service Reform Act of 1978**, passed in response to Watergate, dismantled the Civil Service Commission and created a Merit Systems Protection Board to hear appeals of personnel decisions. It also gave administrative and managerial functions to the Office of Personnel Management.

2. **Constitutional Protection: Property Rights and Procedural Due Process**

   a. *Generally*—The Due Process Clauses of the 5th and 14th amendments state that no person shall be deprived of life, liberty or property without due process of law. This has been interpreted to mean that where government employees have a property interest in their job, the government must provide procedural due process—in the form of notice and an opportunity to be heard—before the employee may be terminated.

   b. *Property Right*—In order for procedural due process rights to be implicated, the employee must have a property interest in his job. Not all government jobs are considered property.

      i. A **property right is found** where a statute, ordinance, or express or implied contract provides for some heightened job security or entitlement to the position. A formal contract may not be necessary if there were other circumstances that led to some guarantee of job security. Teachers with tenure, for example, have a property interest.

ii. The **state may prevent the finding of a property right** by showing that the employee was on probationary or temporary status, or by enacting a statute that defines the job as one without a property interest.

c. *Procedural Due Process*—The Due Process Clause has been interpreted to provide both procedural and substantive rights. Procedural due process—the kind relevant here—does not grant government employees any substantive rights, but only guarantees a fair process for determining whether their property (in this case their job) was improperly taken from them. The two basic requirements of procedural due process in these cases are *notice* and an *opportunity to be heard*.

i. *Notice*—Employees are entitled to be notified of the charges against them, or any other reason for which they are going to be or have been terminated. An oral notification is sufficient.

ii. *Opportunity to be heard*—Employees have the right to a hearing where they may respond to the reasons they have been given for their termination. This does not need to be a full evidentiary hearing with a record and an impartial decision-maker, but may merely be a face-to-face meeting with a superior.

iii. *Amount of due process*—The required elaborateness of the notice and hearing depends on the totality of protections that are offered against unfair dismissal.

d. *State-Action Requirement*—Procedural due process only applies to government employees, although they may work at any level of government—federal, state or local. When a private-sector employee is fired, there is no constitutional right of procedural due process, because the state has not taken the action of firing the employee.

CHAPTER III

EMPLOYEE DUTIES AND OBLIGATIONS

A. Default Rules

1. **Duty of Loyalty**—Employees generally have a "duty of loyalty" to their employers. This obligation is sometimes called a "fiduciary duty." The modern formulation is that unless otherwise agreed, **an employee is subject to a duty to his employer to act solely for the benefit of the employer in all matters connected with his employment.** *Restatement of (Second) of Agency § 387.*

   a. *Nature of the Duty of Loyalty*

      i. *Default rule*—The duty of loyalty is a default rule. That is, it is exists unless the employer and employee change or vitiate it by contract.

      ii. *Relation to employer breach*—The duty of loyalty may not be eliminated by the employer's breach of other contract provisions. For example, if the employer fails to pay an employee a bonus to which that employee is entitled, the employee is not excused from his duty of loyalty. *Jet Courier Service v. Mulei* (Colo. 1989).

      iii. *Remedies*—If the employee is found to have violated the duty of loyalty, the employer generally may recover pay and bonuses for the period during which the employee was not loyal. Other remedies and measures of damages may also apply.

   b. *Employee Competition with Employer*

      i. The duty of loyalty prevents the employee from competing with the employer during the course of his employment.

      ii. *Not a breach*—The following activities are not a breach of the duty of loyalty.

         1) *Preparations*—It is generally not a breach of the duty of loyalty for an employee to *prepare* to compete against his employer, either by searching for another job or by incorporating a business and hiring employees, so long as they are not employees of the current employer.

         2) *Failure to disclose*—The employee is under no obligation to his employer to disclose the fact that he is exploring or preparing to undertake competitive activities.

      iii. *Breach*—Jurisdictions differ on where to draw the line between competition and preparations for competition. But activities which have a present detrimental effect on an employer and which take unfair advantage of the employee's position of trust within the employer-company are usually considered a breach of the duty of loyalty.

    1)   ***Solicitation of co-workers***—Soliciting co-workers to move to the new company is generally a breach of the duty of loyalty.

    2)   ***Solicitation of customers***—Contacting customers and *soliciting* them, that is encouraging them to leave the employer and do business with the employee's new company, is generally a breach of the duty of loyalty.

        a)   ***Solicitation vs. advising***—An employee who merely advises current customers that he may be moving to a competing business is generally not "soliciting" the customers for purposes of the duty of loyalty.

2. Corporate-Opportunities Doctrine—In addition to the duty of loyalty, employees are also constrained by the corporate-opportunities doctrine. High-level employees cannot steal lucrative business opportunities that are **within their employer's current or expected line of business**.

    a. ***Incapability Defense***—If the corporation is financially or legally incapable of taking advantage of the opportunity, the employee may claim a defense.

        i. ***Duty to secure financing***—Courts will sometimes reject a financial incapability defense where it was the duty of the corporate officer to attempt to help raise the capital necessary for the company to be able to take advantage of the opportunity.

        ii. ***Example:*** Bob is the vice president of research & development for MedCo, a medical technology company. An independent inventor comes to Bob proposing a licensing deal for a new artificial heart valve. Bob cannot license the technology himself or through another company in which he has a stake. If, however, MedCo does not have the financial resources to license the product, Bob may be able to take advantage of the deal himself.

B. Employee Breach of Employment Contract

Note: This section is redundant of II.D.1.a.ii.5, but is included here so that this chapter's treatment of employee duties and obligations will be complete.

1. 13th Amendment / No Specific Performance—The 13th Amendment to the U.S. Constitution prohibits slavery and involuntary servitude. This has been interpreted to prevent courts from awarding specific performance (a court order to perform the remainder of the contract) for disputes about personal employment contracts. When an employee breaches an employment contract, the employer is limited to seeking a monetary award.

2. **Calculation of Damages**—If an employee breaches a definite-term contract by quitting before the term has expired, the employer has a duty to mitigate by seeking a replacement worker. In most jurisdictions, the employee can be held liable for the difference between her compensation and the compensation of a replacement worker hired at a higher rate. This difference is the so-called "benefit of the bargain." If the replacement worker's compensation is lower, no damages are recoverable.

   a. *Quit Out of Necessity*—If illness or another "act of God" prevents the employee from completing the contract, performance is excused *by necessity* and no damages are recoverable.

C. Non-Compete Agreements

1. **Explanation**—Non-compete agreements (also called "restrictive covenants" or "covenants not to compete") are contracts in which employees agree that they will not work for competing businesses for a certain period of time after their employment and compensation ends. Most often, these prohibitions are meant to apply even if the employee is fired. Non-compete agreements represent a contractual arrangement that provides stronger protection for the employer than the duty of loyalty or the corporate-opportunities doctrine would alone.

2. **Theory Note**—Some argue that non-compete agreements are anti-competitive because they restrict the free flow of labor. Others contend that because employees enter into the agreements voluntarily, they represent the outcomes of competitive market pressures and employees are therefore compensated for the restriction by higher wages than they would otherwise receive.

3. **Difficult to Enforce**—Contemporary courts are reluctant to enforce non-compete agreements because they often heavily favor the employer without conferring a compensating benefit to the employee. Some states simply refuse to enforce non-compete agreements, declaring them to be against public policy.

4. **Common-law Requirements**—Under the common law, non-compete agreements must have four elements to be enforceable. They must:

   - Serve a legitimate employer interest;

   - Be reasonable in scope and duration (not greater than is necessary to protect the employer interest);

   - Not unduly harm the public interest;

   - Be supported by consideration (sometimes independent) *or* not create undue hardship for the employee

     —Commentators disagree on the formulation of this fourth element.

   a. *Legitimate Employer Interests*—The requirement of serving "legitimate" employer interests narrows the rationales courts will consider in deciding whether a covenant is actionable. It is always within the employer's interest to restrict employees from future competition. Such restrictions aid in the retention of valuable employees and greatly reduce the future bargaining power of employees for raises and perquisites in exchange for staying with the job. Courts do not consider these rationales to be "legitimate" employer interests, however. While courts differ, three categories of employer interest stand out as being more likely to be considered legitimate.

i. ***Protection of trade secrets***—The protection of trade secrets is always a legitimate employer interest. (See also the discussion of trade secrets in III.D, *infra*.)

1) Note that if the employer is claiming the protection of trade secrets as the *only* legitimate employer interest, then the non-compete agreement constitutes little or no protection above and beyond the duty-of-loyalty default rule. Therefore, the courts impose a higher burden for showing reasonability in scope (discussed *infra* at III.C.4.b).

ii. ***Protection of non-trade-secret information***—In most states that allow non-compete agreements, the protection of non-trade-secret information or intangibles such as know-how and goodwill with customers will serve as a legitimate employer interest.

iii. ***Significant investment in specific training***—In some courts non-compete agreements are held to protect a legitimate employer interest when, in the beginning of a worker's tenure, the employer makes a substantial investment in orientation and on-the-job training. During this period, the worker is being compensated more than he is worth, because she spends the balance of time being trained rather than producing. So that employers may recoup their investment in training, this doctrine allows non-compete agreements as necessary to prevent employees from taking unfair advantage of employers.

1) ***General knowledge***—Courts have almost universally held, however, that **general knowledge obtained on the job belongs to the employee**, and the employee cannot be restricted from taking that general knowledge to another employer.

b. ***Reasonableness of Scope and Duration***—Non-compete agreements can be limited by time, geographical area, and/or type of work. In general, the restrictions are not to be greater than those necessary to protect the employer's legitimate interests. There are no hard and fast rules for what restrictions are reasonable. Instead, courts look to the totality of the circumstances.

c. ***Not Unduly Harmful to the Public Interest***—Courts may strike down non-compete agreements if they are significantly harmful to the public interest, such as if they would tend toward the monopolization of trade or would deprive a community of needed professional services.

    d. ***Undue Hardship on the Employee***—Courts may strike down a non-compete agreement if it creates undue hardship on the employee, such as if it would deprive a family of the income it needs to survive or would prevent a person from practicing her chosen profession.

    e. ***Supported by Consideration***—Consideration is not normally an issue for new employees, or continuing employees who receive independent consideration for signing a non-compete. For an ongoing at-will employee who is made to sign a non-compete agreement, however, the courts are split as to whether continued employment constitutes sufficient consideration.

5. **Statutes**—Some states have enacted statutes to deal with non-compete agreements, either making them unenforceable or regulating their scope.

6. **Enforcing Contracts with Overbroad Non-Compete Agreements**—When a court determines a non-compete agreement to be invalid because it is more restrictive than necessary to serve legitimate employer interests, the court may either:

    a. ***Declare the entire contract unenforceable*** because of the faulty provision, or

    b. ***Enforce the contract without the invalid portion***. When enforcing the contract despite part of it being unenforceable, courts use one of two methods to interpret the remaining contract.

        i. ***The blue-pencil method*** involves striking the offending items of text from the contract and enforcing the remaining document if it forms a complete contract.

        ii. ***The reasonable-alteration rule*** allows the court flexibility in adjusting the terms of the contract to make it enforceable.

7. **Suing the Subsequent Employer**—If an employee subject to a non-compete agreement takes another job, the former employer generally may sue not only the former employee, but also the subsequent employer.

D. Trade Secrets

1. **Definition**—A trade secret is a form of intellectual-property protection for ideas and information. Employers can create trade secrets by contract—exposing the secret only to employees or others who agree not to expose the secret information to outside parties.

    a. Note that companies can often hold information as a trade secret even when they cannot obtain a copyright or patent over the information.

2. **Unprotectible as a Trade Secret**—Under the common law, employees are always entitled to take general knowledge, skills, and experience to another employer. The kind of knowledge that employees can be prohibited from taking with them is relatively narrow. For instance, specific information about a special plastics-manufacturing process may be protectible as a trade secret, but general knowledge of plastics engineering—even if acquired on the job—would not be protectible.

3. **Time of injunction**

   a. *Limited to Duration of Secrecy*—In most jurisdictions, if a former employee divulges a trade secret to the subsequent employer, that company can be enjoined only for as long as the trade secret would have remained a secret. For instance, the injunction will not last longer than it would take to "reverse engineer" the product. Reverse engineering means figuring out how to manufacture a product based on experimenting with a legally acquired finished-product. *Schulenberg v. Signatrol, Inc.* (Ill. 1965).

   b. *Theory notes*—

      i. Some commentators argue that the length of injunction should be longer than the time required to reverse engineer, because extra deterrent is required to off-set the substantial chance that the infringing firm will not be caught. Thus to make the risk calculation neutral, injunctions should be punitive. See Edmund W. Kitch, *The Law and Economics of Rights in Valuable Information*[W] (1980).

      ii. Others argue that trade secrets are often economically inefficient because they stifle competition. Even if trade-secret protection is required for incentivizing innovation, an injunction longer than the time required to reverse engineer is unnecessary and would stifle competition.

4. **Common-Law Remedies**—The monetary reward under the common law for disclosing trade secrets can be measured by lost profits, improperly acquired profits, or a reasonable royalty on the information.

5. **Memorized Customer Lists**—Companies may try to protect customer lists as trade secrets, but in general, a former employee may contact customers of her old employer and solicit their business. Some courts recognize an exception for customer lists that were developed at great expense.

6. **Federal Economic Espionage Act of 1996**—This act makes the misappropriation of trade secrets a criminal offense where the employer:

   a. Took reasonable measures to keep the information secret, and

   b. The information derives independent economic value from being secret.

   Penalties for commercial-purpose misappropriation include up to 10 years in prison for individuals and up to $10 million in fines for organizations.

E. Employee Inventions and Works of Authorship

1. **Inventions**—The rights of the employer and the employee in an invention turn on whether the employee is an *inventive employee* or a *noninventive employee*.

   a. *Inventive Employees*—Inventive employees are those hired, at least in part, to invent for the employer. These employees do not have any rights to their inventions; whether invented on or off the job, the employer retains full title to the inventions of such employees.

b. *Noninventive Employees*—Noninventive employees are those hired to do noninventive tasks. When such employees invent, they retain the full title to their invention.

   i. *Shop right*—If a noninventive employee uses the employer's facilities to create the invention, then the employer may have a nonexclusive license to use the invention.

2. **Assignment-of-Invention Clauses**—Many employers require their noninventive employees to sign agreements whereby all rights in inventions become the property of the employer.

   a. *Requirements for Enforcement*—Courts usually uphold these agreements if they are limited to:

      i. Inventions that relate to the employer's business;

      ii. Inventions that are developed during work hours or using employer facilities.

   b. *Holdover Clauses*—Holdover clauses require employees to assign rights in inventions developed after the employment relationship has ended. Employers' rationale for this practice is that employees may secretly stockpile ideas and inventions and wait until the employment ends before developing and profiting from them. Courts will balance the interests of the employer and employee and will usually uphold these clauses if they are reasonable in duration and scope.

3. **Works of Authorship**

   a. *Work-for-Hire Doctrine*—The default rule for determining the ownership of copyright is the work-for-hire doctrine. Under the doctrine, an employer retains the copyright for all copyrightable works created by the employee in the performance of the employee's duties.

   b. *Off-the-Job*—Even if employees are hired to create copyrightable works in the course of their job, works created off-the-job are not owned by the employer.

CHAPTER IV

PRIVACY, EXPRESSION, AND AFFILIATION RIGHTS

A. Rights in the Public Sector vs. the Private Sector

1. **Introduction**—The rights employees have to speak their mind or keep private their personal affairs and possessions are radically different depending on whether their employer is a government entity or a private actor. Government employees, whether federal, state, or local, have federal constitutional rights—such as free speech, due process, equal protection, and privacy—to assert against their employer. Employees of non-governmental entities do not. Government employees also have additional statutory protections that do not apply to employees in the private sector.

2. **The State-Action Requirement for Constitutional Rights**—The Constitution generally does not protect private employees from their employers because of the state-action requirement. For the most part, constitutional rights do not guarantee citizens' abilities to do anything, but merely restrict the ability of the government to take certain actions against its citizens. Thus, it is generally the case that for constitutional rights to be relevant in a dispute, the claimant is required to show that the state caused the contested action—hence the name "state-action requirement."

3. **Exceptions: When Constitutional Rights are Applicable to Private Employees**—There are some ways in which the Constitution affects the rights of private-sector employees. Among them:

   a. **13th Amendment**—The state-action requirement is inapplicable to the 13th Amendment, because the 13th Amendment directly prohibits involuntary servitude rather than merely restricting government power to carry it out.

   b. **Government Mandate**—If the government mandates a certain employer action, the constitutional rights of employees can be implicated.

   c. **Inspiring Development of the Common Law and Statutory Schemes**—Constitutional rights have served as models for the development of law that creates similar protections for private employees.

      i. ***The* Novosel *Case*—In *Novosel v. Nationwide Insurance* (3d Cir. 1983), the court held that an employee discharged for expressing his opinions—an action against the spirit of the First Amendment—could sue his employer in tort. (For more on the *Novosel* case, see IV.C.2.a.i.)

B. Rights of Public Employees

- *N.B.: Rights under this subsection may be implicated for private employees if the employer's conduct was government mandated.*

- *Constitutional due-process protections against termination are covered supra at II.I.2.*

1. **Political Affiliation**—Under the First Amendment, decisions to hire, promote, or discharge an employee cannot be based on political affiliation, unless the employee is in a high policymaking job.

    a. ***Supreme Court Pedigree***—*Elrod v. Burns* (U.S. 1976) and *Branti v. Finkel* (U.S. 1980) established that discharging government employees on the basis of their political affiliations is unconstitutional. *Rutan v. Republican Party* (U.S. 1990) extended that rationale to decisions to hire or promote employees.

2. **Political Activity**—Government employees are both restricted and protected in their political activity by statute. Federally, **the Hatch Act** provides that federal employees cannot run political campaigns or engage in various other activities. Similar state statutes are known as **little Hatch acts**. The constitutionality of little Hatch acts has been upheld. Note that these restrictions function to both restrain speech of government employees and protect their ability to maintain a separate political identity from their superiors.

3. **Free Speech**—Public employees' speech is protected by the First Amendment.

    a. **Pickering** *Three-Part Test*—*Pickering v. Board of Education* (U.S. 1990) sets forth a three-part test to determine whether the speech is protected:

        1. The speech must be on a **matter of public concern**;

        2. The employee's interest in the speech, as a citizen, **must outweigh the government's interest**, as an employer, in the efficient operation of the workplace;

        3. The protected speech must have been a **motivating factor** in the discharge.

        In *Pickering*, a school teacher criticized the school board's proposals for financing school construction. The speech was on a matter of public concern, and therefore the teacher was unconstitutionally terminated.

    b. ***Explanation of Public Concern in* Connick**—In *Connick v. Myers* (U.S. 1983), an assistant district attorney circulated a survey in the workplace about compensation and job security. The Court upheld her termination saying that **the public-concern portion of the *Pickering* test was not to be treated as a threshold inquiry**. The Court noted that the survey touched on issues of public concern but determined the survey to be primarily an employee grievance about office policy. Considered in the overall balance, the Court held, the speech was not constitutionally protected.

    c. ***Application in* Rankin**—McPherson, who did clerical work in a constable's office, was fired for saying after the assassination attempt on President Ronald Reagan: "If they go for him again, I hope they get him." In a 5-4 decision, the court held that the constable had violated the First Amendment in discharging McPherson. The Court found McPherson's speech to be of public concern, and because she worked in a back room where few could hear her, the government interest in limiting her speech was minimal. *Rankin v. McPherson* (U.S. 1987).

   d. *Burdens of Proof*—Initially, the burden is on the employee to show that the speech was a motivating factor in the discharge. After making this showing, however, the employer may assert the defense that the discharge would have occurred anyway.

4. Free Association—The First Amendment's guarantee of freedom of association and expression has been held to provide protection to government employees against compulsory disclosure of membership in, and contributions to, organizations and associations.

   a. *The* **Shelton** *Case*—In *Shelton v. Tucker* (U.S. 1960), an Arkansas law conditioned employment for teachers upon their written disclosure of organizations of which they were members or to whom they were contributors. The Court found this to be unconstitutional.

   b. *Permitted Intrusions*—Requiring disclosure of organizational affiliation is permitted where relevant to the function of the governmental agency. For instance, employees holding FBI-issued security clearances may be required to provide information on affiliations. There are constitutional limits on the extent of the intrusion, however.

   c. *Defense*—The government employer may assert the defense that the discharge would have occurred anyway.

5. Privacy Rights and Drug Testing—Mandatory drug testing of federal employees, such as with the use of urine samples, implicates the Fourth Amendment's protections against unreasonable searches and seizures. Drug testing is permissible, however, where it is not "unreasonable."

   a. *The* **VonRaab** *Case*—*National Treasury Employees Union v. VonRaab* (U.S. 1989) upheld the administration of mandatory drug tests to Customs Service officers, in part because they interdict drugs smuggled across borders. This job function established a special interest in ensuring that the officers are not drug users. The Court hinted that drug testing for non-law-enforcement personnel in the Customs Service—an issue not before the Court—might be unreasonable under the Fourth Amendment.

      i. *The* **Skinner** *Case*—In *Skinner v. Railway Labor Executives Association* (U.S. 1989), decided on the same day as *VonRaab*, the Court held that federally mandated testing of privately employed railway-workers implicated the Fourth Amendment, but was "reasonable" and therefore not unconstitutional. The Court noted that the record specified instances of drug-abusing engineers involved in accidents.

   b. *Random and Periodic Testing*—The courts are split on whether government-mandated drug testing on a random and periodic basis is constitutional.

6. **Privacy Rights and Searches**—The Fourth Amendment provides some protection to government workers from searches in the workplace through its prohibition on "unreasonable searches and seizures."

   a. *The O'Connor Case*—*O'Connor v. Ortega* (U.S. 1987) is the leading case on the application of the Fourth Amendment to searches of government employees. In *O'Connor*, a government physician was under investigation for sexual harassment and for improperly acquiring a computer. The desk and file cabinets in his office were searched.

      i. *Balancing test*—The *O'Connor* case requires courts to perform a balancing test comparing the employee's interest in privacy and the government's interest in the efficient operation of the workplace.

   b. *Reasonable Expectation of Privacy*—The Fourth Amendment is implicated where there is a "reasonable expectation of privacy," and does not depend upon property interests. Therefore, the government may not search an employee's locker merely because the government owns the locker.

      i. The determination of a "reasonable expectation of privacy" has **subjective** and **objective** components.

         1) *Subjective*—The employee must in fact have a subjective belief that the location at issue is private and is not subject to search.

         2) *Objective*—The expectation of privacy that the employee holds must be objectively reasonable under the circumstances, i.e., from society's point of view.

            a) The relevant time for determining the reasonableness of the search is at the inception of the search. In other words, a search is not made reasonable by the subsequent discovery of contraband.

      ii. *Defeating a reasonable expectation of privacy*—Several facts can work to defeat the claim of a reasonable expectation of privacy, including: waiver of rights, abandonment of property, knowledge of a supervisor's possession of keys and/or combinations, workplace regulations allowing searches, and workplace customs.

   c. *Search Must Be Reasonable at Inception and in Scope*—The search must be reasonable under the circumstances in two ways.

      i. *Inception*—When the search is begun, it must be reasonable in the sense that the government must have a legitimate need to conduct the search in order to carry out the supervision, control, and efficient operation of the workplace.

      ii. *Scope*—Even if it is reasonable for a search to be carried out, the search may become unconstitutional if it is unreasonable in scope.

d. *Warrant Unnecessary*—The reasonableness of searches conducted on government employees faces a different standard than the one for law-enforcement searches of citizens. A warrant is not necessary for searches conducted when the government is acting as an employer.

7. **Off-Work Conduct**

a. *Due Process*—If an employee is discharged or disciplined because of off-hours conduct, he or she can raise a constitutional challenge on the basis of **due process**. The constitutional implications of due process include the prohibition of laws that are so vague that citizens do not have adequate warning of what conduct is prohibited. Such laws are said to be "**void for vagueness**." The disposition of off-work-conduct cases has varied widely, but the cases generally separate along the lines of how egregious the conduct of the employee was and how unfair the reason for discharge or discipline seems to be.

    i. It is unclear whether sanctions short of dismissal, such as demotion or transfer, are subject to due-process requirements. See, e.g., *Brown v. Brienan* (7th Cir. 1983) (fearing that due process, thus construed, could swallow state contract law).

b. *Lloyd-Lafollete Act of 1912*—Federal employees have an additional federal statutory protection under the Lloyd-Lafollete Act of 1912, which requires that **the discharge of a federal employee must promote the "efficiency of the service."** Thus, there must be a **sufficient nexus** between the off-hours conduct and the workplace.

C. Rights of Private Sector Employees

N.B.: The "civil rights" of private-sector employees receive spotty protection from a variety of legal claims. In following the organizational principle of the casebooks, the substance of this section is organized by fact pattern rather than legal claim. Because organization by legal claims, however, is likely to be more helpful when answering an exam hypothetical question, a checklist of legal claims precedes the substantive discussion.

1. **Legal Claims**—The following is a non-exhaustive list of legal claims that may be relevant to a lawsuit based on an invasion of employees' privacy, or restriction of their expression or association. (The claims are discussed *infra*, with the exception of discrimination claims, which are discussed in Chapter V. Additional discussion of wrongful-discharge and emotional-distress tort claims and contract claims may be found in Chapter II.)

    i. Torts:

        1) Wrongful discharge in violation of public policy

        2) Intentional infliction of emotional distress

        3) Invasion of privacy

          a)   Intrusion upon seclusion

          b)   Disclosure of private information

      4)   Defamation

ii.   Contracts:

      1)   Express (written or oral) contracts

      2)   Employee handbooks

iii.   Federal statutes:

      1)   National Labor Relations Act (concerted-activity protections)

      2)   Omnibus Crime Control and Safe Streets Act of 1968 (wiretapping prohibition)

      3)   Electronic Communications Privacy Act of 1986

iv.   Federal and state statutes dealing with discrimination, including:

      1)   Title VII of the Civil Rights Act of 1964

      2)   Americans with Disabilities Act of 1990

      3)   Age Discrimination in Employment Act of 1967

2. On-the-Job Protections for Employees

a. ***Free Expression and Association***—Because of the state-action requirement, the First Amendment does not provide for a right to free speech that can be asserted against private-sector employers. Two legal doctrines, however, can sometimes be used to assert protection of free expression in the workplace: the tort of wrongful discharge in violation of public policy (WDVPP) and the protection for concerted activity under the NLRA.

    i.   ***Tort of wrongful discharge in violation of public policy***—It is possible for a WDVPP claim to go forward based on a public policy of free expression. In *Novosel v. Nationwide Insurance* (3d Cir. 1983), a court held that the tort of wrongful discharge may lie for violation of freedom of expression because freedom of expression is an important public policy according to the First Amendment and the Pennsylvania Constitution. In *Novosel*, employees were instructed to obtain signatures to lobby the state legislature on a pending bill. The court held that **a balancing test should compare employee and employer interests**.

        1)   ***Right not to speak***—In *Chavez v. Manville Products* (N.M. 1989), a worker was fired for complaining when his name was added without consent to a letter sent to a U.S. senator urging passage of a bill having to do with asbestos. The firing was held to have violated a clear public policy, creating a claim for WDVPP.

2) ***Limitations on WDVPP for free speech***—Even if WDVPP can be used to protect free expression as a public policy, the tort does not provide the breadth or protection that the First Amendment does. For instance, the higher up the employee is, and the more responsibility with which he is charged, the greater the employer interest will be in the balancing test. In *Korb v. Raytheon* (Mass. 1991), a high-ranking employee of a defense contractor was quoted in the *Washington Post* as criticizing the national-defense budget. The employee was not protected by WDVPP.

ii. ***NLRA protections for concerted activity***—The National Labor Relations Act protects certain kinds of speech related to unionizing. NLRA § 7 and § 8(a)(1) protect "concerted" activity "for the purpose of mutual aid or protection." The protections apply regardless of whether the workplace is unionized, or whether the employee has a conscious goal of unionizing the workplace. *Timekeeping Systems Inc.* (NLRB 1997).

1) **Three-prong test**—For action to be protected by the NLRA, it must be:

a) ***Concerted***—The action must involve preparation for group activity undertaken for "mutual aid or protection," and cannot be merely an individual acting solely on his or her own behalf. Asserting statutory rights, without more, is not "concerted."

b) ***Work-related***—The action must be reasonably related to wages, hours, or other terms and conditions of employment. Circulating a memo to support an increase in the federal minimum wage passes this test, even though the minimum wage was not directly under the employer's control. *Eastex, Inc. v. NLRB* (U.S. 1978).

c) ***Protected***—The action may be unprotected if unlawful, violent, in breach of contract, or indefensible. Distributing handbills to the public disparaging the company's product without referencing an ongoing labor dispute was indefensible and therefore unprotected. *NLRB v. IBEW Local 1129* (U.S. 1953).

2) ***The* Timekeeping Systems *Case:*** An employee sent a "flippant" e-mail to all other employees accusing his boss of misrepresenting the mathematical calculations in determining whether a new vacation policy would result in more days off for the employees. The e-mail was an impermissible basis for discharge. *Timekeeping Systems Inc.* (NLRB 1997).

iii. ***Protection of freedom of expression through whistleblower laws and antiretaliation provisions***—Some employee expression may be protected by the application of whistleblower laws or the antiretaliation provisions of other laws, including discrimination laws. (See Chapter II and Chapter V for further discussion.)

b. **Privacy**

    i.   ***Invasion of privacy torts***—The common-law tort of wrongful invasion of privacy can be applied to protect employees from having their privacy interests invaded by their employer. There are four branches of the "right to privacy":

- Intrusion upon seclusion—A highly offensive intrusion into one's private life.

- False light—Portraying a person to the public in a false light that is highly offensive.

- Right of publicity—The unauthorized use of a person's name, identity, or image for a commercial purpose such as advertising.

- Disclosure of private facts—Dissemination to the public of private facts, where the public disclosure is highly offensive.

The doctrine most analogous to Fourth Amendment protections is intrusion upon seclusion.

    1)   ***Intrusion upon seclusion***—

        a)   **Restatement:** "One who intentionally intrudes, physically or otherwise, upon the solitude or seclusion of another, or his private affairs or concerns, is subject to liability to the other for invasion of his privacy, if the intrusion would be highly offensive to a reasonable person." *Restatement (Second) of Torts* § 652B (1976).

            i)   ***Example***: All employee lockers at a discount store were searched on the suspicion that someone had stolen a watch. An employee's personal combination lock was cracked and the contents of her purse were searched. The invasion was an actionable tort. *K-Mart Corp. Store No. 7441 v. Trotti* (Tex. App. 1984).

            ii)   ***Opening "personal" mail***—Where an employer opened mail marked "personal" for an employee, the employee had a claim for invasion of privacy. *Vernars v. Young* (3d Cir. 1976).

    ii.   ***Omnibus Crime Control and Safe Streets Act of 1968***—This federal statute generally prohibits "wiretapping," i.e., the interception of private telephone communications.

        1)   ***Business exception***—The statue excepts listening-in if it is "in the ordinary course of ... business."

a) Tapping an employee's phone based on the suspicion that the employee is disclosing confidential information can fall under the business exception. *Briggs v. American Air Filter* (5th Cir. 1980).

b) "In the ordinary course" does not mean "anything that interests a company." Tapping a phone to determine if an employee is looking for another job is not excepted. *Watkins v. L.M. Berry & Co.* (11th Cir. 1983).

2) ***Consent voids 'wiretapping'***—If the parties to the phone call are aware that the conversation is being recorded or listened to, then there is generally no wiretapping, because the conversation is not 'private.'

iii. ***State wiretapping statutes***—States have their own statutes on wiretapping and recording telephone conversations. States differ, however, on whether only one party or all parties to the conversation need to consent to recording the conversation.

iv. ***The Electronic Communications Privacy Act of 1986***—This federal statute bans the interception or disclosure of electronic communications. The law contains an "ordinary course of business" exception, however, specifically allowing the monitoring of computer terminals for work performance.

3. Off-Duty Employee Conduct Protections

a. ***Political Activity***

i. ***State laws protecting public office seekers***—Many states have laws prohibiting interference with persons' candidacy for public office. In *Davis v. Louisiana Computing* (La. App. 1981), such a law was used where a worker was fired for running for city council.

b. ***Freedom of Association***

i. ***Discharge law***—Tort or contract-based discharge actions can be used as claims where employees were fired because of their associations.

1) ***The* Rulon-Miller *Case:*** Virginia Rulon-Miller was an IBM manager who was dating a man working for a rival company. Although an IBM policy stated that employees had a right to privacy in their off-work lives, Rulon-Miller was fired for her "conflict of interest." The court held that she had a claim for wrongful discharge. *Rulon-Miller v. International Business Machines Corp.* (Cal. App. 1984).

ii. ***Intentional infliction of emotional distress (IIED)***—The tort of intentional infliction of emotional distress can be used as a claim where employers cause employees distress because of their associations.

1) ***Elements of IIED***—To make out a claim for IIED, the plaintiff must show that the defendant committed an extreme and outrageous act with the intent to cause severe emotional distress and that the act did indeed cause severe emotional distress.

2) ***The* Rulon-Miller *Case:*** In *Rulon-Miller v. International Business Machines Corp.* (Cal. App. 1984) (discussed in IV.C.3.b.i.1 *supra*), Rulon-Miller was given a choice of leaving her boyfriend or quitting her job. The next day she was fired. Her supervisor said he was "making the decision for [her]." A jury found that the supervisor had sought to make Rulon-Miller feel powerless and oppressed, allowing a verdict for IIED in addition to wrongful discharge.

iii. ***Discrimination law***—If the employer takes adverse action against an employee because of the protected status of another person with whom that employee is associating, then the employee may have a claim under discrimination law. For instance, if an employee were refused a job or fired because he had a relationship with someone who was HIV positive or who was of a certain race, that action would constitute discrimination under the ADA or Title VII, respectively.

c. ***Off-Duty Activities***

i. ***Tort of wrongful discharge in violation of public policy***—The tort of wrongful discharge can occasionally be used to protect workers from discharge based on those workers' off-hours activities. The key to stating a cause of action for the tort of wrongful discharge is showing a public policy that is threatened by the discharge. (See II.F.)

1) ***The* Brunner *Case:*** An employee at an auto-body shop did volunteer work with AIDS patients. She was fired out of a concern that she might spread AIDS to shop employees, even though she did not have AIDS herself. The court found no cause of action for wrongful termination, narrowly construing "public policy," and finding that "encouraging volunteer work" does not sustain the tort. *Brunner v. Al Attar* (Tex. App. 1990).

4. **Employer Acquisition of Employee Information**—Employers often seek to learn a tremendous amount of private, sensitive information about their employees. For the most part, employers are free to acquire such information as they like. There are, however, some legal doctrines that can be used in certain circumstances that may be applied to prevent or remedy some information gathering.

a. ***Application of Discrimination Law***—Various discrimination laws may provide a cause of action with regard to specific questions an interviewer asks, or specific information an employer seeks, if that information is related to protected statuses. Inquiring about a person's racial, religious, disability, or pregnancy status may run afoul of discrimination laws.

b. ***Polygraphs***—A polygraph device, or "lie detector," is used to measure signs of anxiety that a person may experience during questioning. The measurements are used to determine the likelihood that someone is lying.

    i.   ***Employee Polygraph Protection Act of 1988 (EPPA)***—This federal law prohibits directly or indirectly making an employee or employment-applicant submit to a polygraph test. The law also bans use of the results of such a test.

    ii.   ***Enforcement***—Employees may sue under the law, and civil penalties are authorized.

    iii.   ***Exemptions:***

        1)   ***Certain employers***—Some whole categories of employers are excluded from the prohibition against polygraph usage, including public employers, defense contractors, drug manufacturers, and security firms.

        2)   ***"On-going" investigation exemption***—Any employer may ask an employee to submit to a polygraph in the course of investigating a theft, but the employer is required to follow procedural guidelines.

    iv.   ***Effect on state law***—The EPPA does not preempt more restrictive state laws.

c. ***Paper-and-Pencil Honesty Testing***—Because of the general prohibition on polygraph testing, many employers have used psychologist-designed "paper-and-pencil" tests to measure honesty, personality, and psychological traits.

    i.   ***Generally legal***—There are no blanket prohibitions against paper-and-pencil testing, except in Massachusetts, where a statute restricts employers from administering the tests. The legal status of the tests is doubtful in California.

    ii.   ***Invasion of privacy***—In at least one state, California, an applicant may contest paper-and-pencil testing as an invasion of privacy under state-constitution-based civil rights. The leading case is *Sokora*:

        1)   ***The* Soroka *Case:*** The court held that the use of the Psychscreen test violated the state-constitutional rights of security-officer applicants at Target Stores. The court found that questions about religious beliefs and sexual orientation were not related to job performance. *Soroka v. Dayton-Hudson* (Cal. App. 1991).

        2)   ***Requirements***—Justification of an invasion of the applicant's privacy under the California Constitution requires:

            a)   ***Compelling interest***—An invasion of the applicant's privacy must be justified under a compelling-interest standard, a higher standard than the federal Constitution's "reasonable" standard.

      b)   ***Nexus requirement***—The private information sought must be related to job performance.

      c)   Note that there is no state-action requirement for this state constitutional right.

     3)   ***Limitation on*** **Sokora**—The holding of *Sokora* may be limited by *Loder v. City of Glendale* (Cal. 1997), in which the California high court held that the City of Glendale could not conduct drug testing on incumbent employees, but that the city could conduct suspicionless drug tests on applicants. The court held that with applicants there is a lesser invasion of privacy than with incumbents.

   iii.   ***Specific questions***—Specific questions on a paper-and-pencil test may be actionable under federal or state discrimination law.

  d. ***Genetic Testing***—A significant minority of states prohibit genetic testing. Title VII and the ADA may also allow causes of action for genetic testing. HIPAA prohibits the use of genetic testing for denying coverage to an employee in a group health plan.

  e. ***Drug Testing***—There are no general bans on drug testing of employees.

    i.   ***Restrictions on random testing***—A minority of states restrict random testing, allowing tests only when there is a reasonable suspicion or probable cause that a particular employee is under the influence of drugs.

    ii.   ***Restrictions on use of results***—A minority of states restrict how employers can use the positive results. Some states have requirements for confidentiality, re-testing, and limits on what disciplinary action can be taken.

   iii.   ***False positives and the ADA***—Persons discriminated against because of the false belief that they are drug users may have a claim for discrimination under the ADA.

5. Employer Disclosure of Employee Information—Employers may disclose information about their employees for the purpose of giving references or for other reasons.

  a. ***Defamation***—The tort of defamation protects persons against malicious and injurious lies told about them. Defamation is often called "slander" if it is spoken and "libel" if it is written.

    i.   ***Elements***—To make out a case for defamation, the plaintiff must show:

     1)   ***False and defamatory statement***—There must have been a false and defamatory statement concerning the plaintiff;

     2)   ***Unprivileged publication***—The statement must have been published—that is communicated—to a third party without the protection of any privilege;

3) *Negligence or higher standard of fault*—The publisher's fault must amount to at least negligence, and

4) *Special harm, if necessary*—Libel and some kinds of slander, including oral statements concerning the person's business or trade, do not require a showing of special harm. Other slander, however, may require a showing of special harm to the plaintiff.

    a) Satisfying the special harm element is usually not an issue in employment defamation cases, since the statement is usually concerning the person's business or trade.

ii. *Implication and opinion can be actionable*—A statement does not have to be directly negative, nor must it be a plain statement of fact. If the statement communicates a misleading and damaging impression of the employee, the statement may be actionable.

    1) *The* **Stanbury** *Case:* An employee, Stanbury, was terminated from Sigal Construction Co. An employer with whom Stanbury applied called Sigal for a reference. Littman, who had never worked with Stanbury directly, said Stanbury was "detail oriented" and that he couldn't see "the big picture." Sigal later conceded these statements were false. After being rejected for the job, Stanbury sued. The court held that a jury could find that the statements were defamatory, because they could be found to have implied that Stanbury was a poor employee, and because Littman's opinion, which was offered without first-hand knowledge, could be regarded as reckless. *Sigal Construction Corp. v. Stanbury* (D.C. App. 1991).

iii. *Constitutional limitations on defamation*—Although not usually relevant to the employment-law context, it should be noted that the First Amendment has been interpreted to place certain limitations on defamation claims where the speech involved touches on a matter of public concern or where the plaintiff is a public figure.

b. *Invasion of Privacy*—Disclosing information of a private and personal nature may constitute tortious invasion of privacy. For example, disclosure of medical-records kept by the employer could constitute invasion of privacy.

c. *Intentional Infliction of Emotional Distress*—If the disclosure of information is extreme and outrageous and causes severe emotional distress, there may be a cause of action under IIED.

CHAPTER V

DISCRIMINATION

A. Introduction

Employment discrimination law does not prohibit employers from taking any action against their employees. The laws of discrimination only—but not always—prohibit conduct when it is *because of* a person's status, such as the person's race, gender, or age. To prove that the action was "because of" the person's status, the plaintiff must show discriminatory intent ("disparate treatment"), discriminatory effect ("disparate impact"), or that the employer failed to reasonably accommodate the employee's differences ("reasonable accommodation"). Remember that discrimination law offers no general protection against employer practices—no matter how onerous or unfair— unless they are connected to a treatment differential between employees of one status and those of another. Note that only a few of the many possible statuses are protected, and of those that are protected, some are more protected than others. Finally, you will see that not all discrimination against protected statuses is illegal: Employers may discriminate when—under the eyes of the law—they have a good reason to do so. Although most classwork focuses on federal discrimination law, state law often picks up where federal law has left off, reaching employers, employees, and kinds of discrimination that are not covered by federal statute.

> *FOR BETTER UNDERSTANDING:* Understanding a few basic terms and concepts about discrimination law and how it is organized for classroom teaching will speed your understanding of the material:
>
> **What is meant by "status"?** A "status" is the quality or characteristic that forms the basis upon which people discriminate. Statuses include age, race, gender, religion, national origin, disability status, pregnancy status, and even other things such as whether or not a person is a union member or how educated someone is. Some commentators refer to "status discrimination" rather than "discrimination." In practice, adding the word "status" to "discrimination" is superfluous. Non-status discrimination would simply be perceiving and acting on differences between people based on highly individual factors—factors too unique to be considered a "status." Of course, this kind of "discrimination" is not only legal, it describes every personnel decision ever made. In fact, most "status discrimination" is also legal. Discrimination only becomes problematic when it is because of a "protected status," such as race.
>
> **What is meant by a "class"?** A "class" is a description of someone's status. Native Americans, for example, form a class that is sometimes discriminated against. "Women," "whites," and "Jews" are classes for the statuses of gender, race and religion, respectively.

Beware: _Despite the fact that the definitions of "class" and "status" are distinct, some writers and professors use the terms interchangeably._

What is a "model" or "theory" of discrimination? A "model" or "theory" of discrimination is a broad category of how one goes about proving that discrimination happened. There are three major models: "disparate treatment," "disparate impact," and "reasonable accommodation." Considered along with individual statutes, the models define what is and is not actionable discrimination.

Why discuss the models first? This outline follows the prevalent classroom practice of first discussing the models of discrimination, and then discussing the protected statuses, such as race, gender, disability status, and their accompanying legal bases—Title VII, the ADA, and so forth. This can be a counterintuitive and initially confusing way to organize the study employment-discrimination law. Because the models do not apply to all legal claims and all protected statuses in the same way, the more careful and accurate way to review discrimination law would be to go through the individual statutes one at a time, discussing the models as they are relevant to each statute. The advantage of discussing the models on a stand-alone basis up front, however, is that it aids in seeing how all discrimination statutes are similar. But even more importantly, this way of organizing is likely to be more helpful for the exam, since showing that you can apply the strategies developed for one statute to a different statute shows creativity and a conceptual mastery of the law—ultimately more impressive to professors than rote memorization.

B. Proving Discrimination: Legal Models and Theories

1. **Overview**—Theories or models for proving discrimination are very important to discrimination law. While essentially procedural or evidentiary in nature—delineating burdens of proof and production and discussing what evidence is relevant—the models act to define the substantive scope of discrimination law. There are essentially three broad categories of doctrine for proving discrimination, each of which has various subcategories. The original way to prove discrimination is to show discriminatory _intent_; this is called "disparate treatment." The alternative method of proof, called "disparate impact," does not require showing intent or improper motive at all, but focuses on the _effect_ of employment practices. These models for proving discrimination can also be thought of as alternative ways of defining the phrase "because of" in statutes that prohibit conduct _because_ of discrimination." The third model of discrimination is "reasonable accommodation," which involves changing job requirements or physical qualities of the workplace so that members of a protected class can work. Reasonable accommodation comes into play in cases involving religious belief and disability status.

2. **Disparate Treatment**—Establishing disparate treatment requires proving, either directly or indirectly, that the **employer had the *intent* or *improper motive* to discriminate**. There are two major categories of doctrine within disparate treatment: individual disparate treatment and systemic disparate treatment.

    a. *Individual Disparate Treatment*—Individual disparate treatment claims allege that the employer discriminated in an individual case. Evidence can either be direct or created through inference.

        i. *Direct evidence*—Discrimination can be proved by producing statements of an employer that the employer is making an employment decision based someone's race, sex, or some other protected status. In the entertainment business, it is common for employers to specify the sex of a performer, for instance, and if sued, they would assert a BFOQ defense (discussed *infra* at V.B.5). But in most other contexts, where the discrimination is obviously illegal, employers usually do not offer such convenient evidence of their own discriminatory intent.

            1) *The* **Price Waterhouse** *Case:* In an accounting firm, a woman denied partnership was told that to increase her chances of being offered partnership in the future she should "walk more femininely, talk more femininely, dress more femininely, wear make-up, have her hair styled, and wear jewelry." Because the partnership decision resulted from sex-stereotyping, it constituted discrimination under Title VII. *Price Waterhouse v. Hopkins* (U.S. 1989).

            2) *The* **Slack** *Case:* Three black women and one white woman worked in the bonding and coating department of an assembly plant. On a day the workers were required to scrape deposits of hardened resin off the floor, the white worker was excused and replaced with a black worker from another department. A supervisor told one of the black women "colored folks were hired to clean because they clean better." The disparate conditions were discrimination under Title VII. *Slack v. Havens* (S.D. Cal. 1973).

        ii. *Inferential evidence*—Because such "smoking gun" direct evidence of intent is rare, in the *McDonnell Douglas* line of cases the Supreme Court developed a method for proving discrimination by inferring intent from conduct. These cases set out procedural burdens of proof and production.

            1) *Plaintiff's prima facie case*—The requirements for a prima facie case were first developed in *McDonnell Douglas v. Green* (U.S. 1973) and were clarified in *Texas Dept. of Community Affairs v. Burdine* (U.S. 1981). While the factors are usually stated in reference to discrimination in hiring, they can be adapted to discrimination in other terms or conditions of employment. To make out a prima facie case for disparate treatment, the plaintiff has the burden of proof to show that he or she:

a)   Is a member of a protected class;

b)   Was qualified for the job;

c)   Was rejected for the job, and

d)   The job either remained open or was given to someone who is not a member of the protected class.

2)   ***Defendant's burden of production of non-discriminatory reason***—After a prima facie case is established, the defendant merely has the burden of production (not proof) of articulating a non-discriminatory reason for the employment decision. At this stage, if the employer were admitting to discrimination, it could assert a BFOQ defense (discussed *infra* at V.B.5).

3)   ***Plaintiff's burden of proof of pretext***—After the defendant has articulated a non-discriminatory reason, the plaintiff has the burden of proving that the reason is a pretext; that is, that the stated reason is not the *real reason* the plaintiff suffered the negative employment consequence.

a)   ***Finding for the defendant despite pretext***—Under *St. Mary's Honor Center v. Hicks* (U.S. 1993), the plaintiff's proof of pretext is sufficient for rendering a plaintiff's verdict. However, the showing of pretext does not compel a verdict for the plaintiff if it is found that the real reason for the negative employment decision was non-discriminatory. A dissenting opinion to *St. Mary's* criticized the ruling for absolving employers of the responsibility for lying to the courts in producing their original non-discriminatory reason for the employment decision.

iii.   ***Causation issues / mixed-motive cases***—In some cases the factfinder may find that both an impermissible discriminatory motive and a permissible motive were the cause of an employment decision.

1)   ***Price Waterhouse's "but for" causation***—In *Price Waterhouse v. Hopkins* (U.S. 1989), the Supreme Court held that "but for" causation was necessary to establish a violation of Title VII. That is, even if the plaintiff showed that the defendant had an impermissible discriminatory motive in making the employment decision, if the defendant could show that it would have come to the same decision even if it had not had the discriminatory motive, then the defendant would not be liable.

2)   ***Civil Rights Act of 1991***—Partially overruling *Price Waterhouse*, Congress passed the Civil Rights Act of 1991. Section 703(m) of the '91 Act provides that **once the plaintiff has proven that an impermissible factor motivated the employment decision, then the plaintiff has established a violation**. If the defendant can

establish the absence of "but for" causation, i.e., that the defendant would have made the same employment decision even without the discriminatory motive, then the remedies are limited. The plaintiff may not receive any damages in such a case, but may recover attorney's fees and costs. In such situations, the court may also impose an injunction, but not one that specifically benefits the plaintiff, such as a reinstatement order.

b. ***Systemic Disparate Treatment***—In contrast to individual disparate treatment, systemic disparate treatment claims allege a *pattern or practice* of discrimination against a protected class. This can be proven with either direct evidence or circumstantial inference, but the more interesting and difficult doctrinal issues arise with proving systemic disparate impact by inference.

   i. ***Direct evidence***—If a plaintiff produces direct evidence of a policy, pattern, or practice of discrimination, a violation will be established. As with individual disparate treatment, such evidence is rare in cases of obviously illegal discrimination. But where the discrimination is likely to be excused by way of affirmative defenses such as affirmative action or the BFOQ defense (discussed *infra* at V.B.5), then the employer's discriminatory practice is likely to be stated in an up front manner.

   ii. ***Inference by statistics and probability theory***—Without direct evidence, plaintiffs may inferentially establish discrimination using statistics and probability theory.

      1) ***Stark disparities***—In *Teamsters v. United States* (U.S. 1977), the Supreme Court held that statistical disparities for a trucking company were so stark that they could establish a prima facie case. In *Teamsters*, 0.4 percent of the company's drivers were black, yet 5 percent of their non-driver employees were black, and the company hired out of areas such as Atlanta, where 22 percent of the metro population is black.

      2) ***Standard-deviation analysis***—Where statistical discrepancies are not as stark as in *Teamsters*, statistical significance can be an issue. In *Hazelwood School District v. United States* (U.S. 1977), the Supreme Court approved the use of standard-deviation analysis for determining the statistical significance of imbalances between hired workers and the relevant labor pool. The court did not rule on how statistically significant the discrepancy had to be to form a prima facie case of systemic disparate treatment.

         HOW STANDARD-DEVIATION ANALYSIS WORKS: A standard deviation is measure how significant statistical results are, or how likely they are to be the result of pure chance. By inputting the relevant numbers of people hired and those from the relevant labor pool into a mathematical formula, one can find the number of standard deviations. Two standard deviations represents a 5-percent chance that the statistical correlation or discrepancy was caused by randomness. Three standard deviations means that there is a 1-percent chance the correlation or discrepancy was caused by randomness. Therefore, requiring two to three standard deviations for statistical analysis of systemic disparate treatment data would mean requiring a demonstration that it was 95- to 99-percent likely that the discrepancy is the result of real discrimination rather than chance.

3) ***Finding the relevant labor pool for comparison***—The proper labor pool for comparison is all the persons who are ready, willing, and able to work; this includes taking education and experience into account. For low-skill jobs, the labor pool will tend to be local. For higher-skill, higher-paying jobs, the labor pool may be national.

3. **Disparate Impact / Adverse Impact**—In *Griggs v. Duke Power* (U.S. 1971), the Supreme Court interpreted Title VII as allowing claims against employers where there is no showing of intent if the plaintiff can show discriminatory effect. This disparate-impact theory (also called "adverse impact") makes actionable practices that are "fair in form, but discriminatory in operation." Under disparate impact, facially neutral criteria, such as requiring a high school diploma, a minimum height, or a minimum score on a standardized test, can be actionable discrimination if plaintiffs can show that the criteria has a significant adverse effect on a protected class and is not dictated by a business necessity.

a. ***Magnitude of the Disparity***—The Supreme Court has never ruled on the magnitude of disparity that is necessary to establish a prima-facie disparate-impact case. The EEOC, which prosecutes violations of discrimination law, has adopted a four-fifths rule in deciding which cases to prosecute. The four-fifths rule has become a rule of thumb in analyzing disparate-impact cases.

i. ***The Four-Fifths Rule***—According to the four-fifths rule, if the selection criteria of the employer results in a selection rate of a protected class that is 80 percent (four-fifths) or less of the selection rate for the allegedly favored group, then the criteria fails the four-fifths rule.

1) ***Example:*** A job requires applicants to yell into a decibelmeter, which measures the loudness of their voices, and reach a level of 100 decibels to be eligible for the job. If 50 percent of men pass the test, but only 40 percent of women do, then the pass rate for women is 80 percent of the pass rate for men, and the test fails the four-fifths rule.

b. ***The Business-Necessity Defense***—Once a prima facie case for disparate impact has been made, the employer can assert an affirmative defense by proving that the contested selection criterion is required as a business necessity. The Civil Rights

Act of 1991 made it clear that the employer carries the burden of proof with regard to showing a business necessity. "Business necessity" is a somewhat ambiguous term and is not defined by statute. Requiring a high-school education for coal-handling jobs was held not to be a business necessity. *Griggs v. Duke Power Co.* (U.S. 1971). But requiring a college education for commercial airline pilots was held to be a business necessity because of a concern for public safety, despite the absence of empirical evidence showing that college education was related to flying ability. *Spurlock v. United Airlines* (10th Cir. 1972).

    i.   ***The* Griggs *Case:*** Candidates for jobs as coal handlers or other low-skill positions were required to be high-school graduates to be eligible for selection. The high-school-education requirement was shown to have an adverse disparate impact on black applicants as compared to whites. Because a high-school education for coal handling and other jobs could not be shown to be a business necessity, the disparate-impact claim could go forward. *Griggs v. Duke Power* (U.S. 1971).

  c. ***Less Discriminatory Alternatives***—Where business necessity justifies the use of contested selection criteria, a plaintiff can still prevail by demonstrating that other selection processes that have a "lesser discriminatory effect" could also suitably serve the business needs of the employer. *Watson v. Fort Worth Bank & Trust* (U.S. 1988).

    i.   Note that the Supreme Court altered this doctrine in *Wards Cove Packing Co. v. Antonio* (U.S. 1989), but the subsequent Civil Rights Act of 1991 overruled the Supreme Court's decision, making previous jurisprudence the controlling authority.

  d. ***Particular Practice vs. Bottom-Line Discrimination***—In *Wards Cove Packing Co. v. Antonio* (U.S. 1989), the Supreme Court held that a plaintiff may not merely prove a "bottom-line" imbalance between the protected class and members of other classes, but must prove that a particular practice was causing the discriminatory impact. The Civil Rights Act of 1991 partially overruled this, however, by allowing plaintiffs to prevail with a showing of "bottom-line" discriminatory impact if they could show that the elements of the selection process could not be separated for analysis.

4. Reasonable Accommodation—While disparate treatment and disparate-impact theories are concerned with what employers *must not do* to workers on the basis of their status, reasonable accommodation is concerned with what employers *must do* for their employees based on their status. In fact, reasonable accommodation often requires treating different people differently, rather than treating all people the same; it therefore represents a departure from the traditional idea of discrimination. "Reasonable accommodation" means changing something about the workplace or the way in which people may work so that people of various religious beliefs or people with disabilities can do a job.

a. *Accommodation*—Accommodations may include restructuring work schedules, changing work practices, changing characteristics of services offered to employees, or purchasing special equipment.

b. *Reasonable*—Not all accommodations must be made—only those that are "reasonable." The definition of "reasonable" differs between religion (Title VII) and disability (Rehabilitation Act / ADA). In general, however, accommodations may be unreasonable when they are tremendously expensive compared to their effectiveness. An accommodation is not necessary to bring working conditions for protected-class workers into absolute identity with working conditions for other workers. Additionally, an employer may choose the accommodation to be offered and does not need to obey the employee's preference.

c. *Affirmative Defense: Undue Hardship*—The exact meaning of "undue hardship" also depends on whether the case involves religion or disability. In general, however, it allows employers to escape the duty to provide reasonable accommodation where it would have a substantial negative effect on the employer, e.g., requiring the employer to significantly change the way it does business, or causing severe financial harm to the employer.

   i. *Undue hardship vs. reasonability*—Undue hardship is distinct from the reasonability requirement. A very large company with tremendous financial resources, for instance, will have an extremely difficult time proving undue hardship, since such a company could easily absorb the accommodation. The same company may, however, use reasonability to avoid making easy and inexpensive changes if they would do very little to help a member of a protected class.

5. **Affirmative Defenses**—Certain affirmative defenses are generally applicable regardless of the model of discrimination used.

   a. *Bona-Fide Occupational Qualification (BFOQ)*—The BFOQ defense is appropriate when an employer *admits* that it discriminated on the basis of the protected status, but believes it had a compelling reason to do so.

      i. *Examples of usage*—The BFOQ is what allows the Catholic Church to discriminate against Protestants and Jews when hiring clergy. The BFOQ allows Hollywood studios to insist on having a woman play the role of Lady Macbeth, and it allows advertising agencies to hire only men for modeling neckties. The BFOQ defense can also make mandatory retirement ages legal for positions such as airline pilots. Notably, the BFOQ is not available for race-discrimination.

      ii. *Narrow exception*—While the BFOQ defense is important in legalizing a tremendous amount of common and largely uncontroversial employer discrimination practices, in *Dothard v. Rawlinson* (U.S. 1977), the BFOQ was described by the Supreme Court as an "extremely narrow exception," which could not be founded upon "stereotyped characterizations."

iii. ***Customer preferences***—The BFOQ cannot ordinarily be used merely because customers prefer to deal with employees who are of a certain sex, age, religion, or other protected status. In *Wilson v. Southwest Airlines* (N.D. Tex. 1981), the airline was not permitted to use the BFOQ defense to hire only female flight attendants despite a marketing technique directed at male travelers that called for the cultivation of a "love" image. The court held that sex appeal was not essential to the primary function of an airline. Hiring only women for exotic-dancer positions in a striptease club, however, would be defensible on the basis of BFOQ.

b. ***Voluntary Affirmative-Action Plans***—Affirmative action is deliberate discrimination in employer decisions that is designed to remedy harmful past discrimination against a certain group.

> ***FOR BETTER UNDERSTANDING:*** Affirmative action is relevant to employment-discrimination law in two different ways. As discussed here, voluntary affirmative-action plans may be initiated by the employer, and then used **as a defense** when a person disadvantaged by the program sues. Alternatively, affirmative action may be used **as a remedy**; courts may order employers to implement affirmative-action programs in order to correct patterns and practices of discrimination that have resulted in an unbalanced workforce.

i. ***Use as a defense***—Voluntary affirmative-action plans may be asserted as a defense to suits brought by members of an *unprotected class*.

1) ***Example:*** If a white person is denied a promotion because an affirmative action plan results in the hiring of a black person, the white person may sue under Title VII, but the prima facie violation will be excused if the employer can establish that the decision was the result of a proper affirmative-action plan.

ii. ***"Reverse discrimination"***—Discrimination against members of a non-minority or unprotected class is sometimes called "reverse discrimination," because it is against the group traditionally favored by what is called "invidious discrimination."

iii. ***Requirements for validity***—Not all affirmative action is allowed under discrimination laws. The affirmative action must be carried out as a plan to attain a balanced workforce, remedying a conspicuous or manifest imbalance between groups of a protected status.

1) ***The remedial requirement***—The affirmative action program must be *remedial*, that is, it **must be designed to "attain, not maintain"** an equitable balance in the workforce on the basis of race or other status.

2) ***The plan requirement***—Only affirmative action that is part of a "plan" will serve as a defense. Ad-hoc affirmative action, in which

employers simply decide on a case-by-case basis to favor one group over another, is not permitted.

C. Title VII of the Civil Rights Act of 1964

1. **Introduction**—The Civil Rights Act of 1964, amended several times since its enactment, is the most comprehensive federal anti-discrimination scheme. The act includes titles dealing with housing, public accommodation, education, and other fields. Title VII, which deals with employment, is the furthest reaching federal statute for employment discrimination on the basis of race, religion, national origin, and sex. Other statutes, such as the Equal Pay Act and Section 1983, overlap to some degree with Title VII, but offer important differences making them very useful to some plaintiffs.

2. **Coverage**

   a. *Covered Employees*— Only "employees" are covered, not shareholders, independent contractors, or other non-employees associated with an employer.

   b. *Covered Employers*—

      i. Only employers in an industry affecting interstate commerce who have 15 or more employees are covered by Title VII.

      ii. *Public employers*—

         1) **State and local governments** are covered as employers under Title VII. Elected officials and appointees to high policymaking government jobs are not counted as "employees" for Title VII, however.

         2) **The federal and District of Columbia governments** are exempted under Title VII's general provisions and covered by an alternative scheme elsewhere in the statute.

      iii. *Religious organizations*—Religious organizations are generally exempted so that they may discriminate based on the religious beliefs of employees or applicants. While there is no exemption for race or gender discrimination in Title VII, the Free Exercise Clause of the First Amendment would probably prevent Title VII from being used by a woman suing a church for not hiring female ministers.

      iv. *Only employers covered*—Title VII does not create a cause of action against supervisors or other individual employees. **Plaintiffs can only sue employers** and similar institutions, such as employment agencies and labor organizations.

         1) *Vicarious liability*—In the context of a sexual-harassment case, *Faragher v. Boca Raton* (U.S. 1998), the Supreme Court held that an employer may be sued for discrimination caused by their

employees, but the **employer may assert an affirmative defense** establishing:

- The employer took reasonable steps to prevent or correct the discrimination, and

- The employee unreasonably failed to avail herself of the preventative and corrective measures the employer offered.

    a)   ***The* Faragher *Case:*** Male lifeguard supervisors for the City of Boca Raton created a "sexually hostile atmosphere" by subjecting Beth Ann Faragher to "uninvited and offensive touching," lewd remarks, and other harassment. Faragher sued. The City argued that it could not be vicariously liable since the harassing behavior was "outside the scope" of the lifeguard's employment. Faragher prevailed because the supervisors were granted virtually unchecked authority over the Faragher and other employees, and those employees were isolated from other, higher-ranking city employees. *Faragher v. Boca Raton* (U.S. 1998).

3. Prohibited Conduct—

a. ***Section 703(a)(1)*** contains Title VII's centerpiece prohibition, making it unlawful "to fail or refuse to hire or to discharge ... or otherwise to discriminate against any individual with respect to his compensation, terms, conditions, or privileges of employment because of such individual's **race, color, religion, sex or national origin**."

b. ***Section 703(a)(2)*** attempts nip some discrimination in the bud by making it **unlawful** for an employer "**to limit, segregate, or classify his employees** or applicants for employment in any way which would deprive or tend to deprive any individual of employment opportunities or otherwise adversely affect his status as an employee because of ... race, color, religion, sex, or national origin."

c. ***Terms, Conditions, and Privileges***—The broad statutory language goes well beyond discriminatory discharge and hiring and reaches *terms, conditions, and privileges* of employment. This is interpreted to cover situations such as sexual harassment.

4. Protected Statuses—There are a few things to note about the protected statuses.

a. ***Race—***

    i.   ***Protection attaches to status, not class***—All races are protected, including whites, blacks, people of Southeast Asian ancestry, etc. One need not be a member of a racial minority to be protected by Title VII.

    1)   Many **affirmative action** programs, however, are exempt under Title VII (discussed *supra* at V.B.5.b).

ii.   ***Associations with status***—The prohibition on racial discrimination includes discrimination against persons because of the racial character of their associations. For instance, if a white woman were fired because she was dating a black man, the white woman would be protected.

iii.   Race is the only status for which the **BFOQ defense is not available**.

iv.   Racial discrimination is also covered by **§ 1981** (discussed *infra* at V.D).

b.   ***Sex***—

    i.   ***Pregnancy Discrimination Act of 1979***—With the passage of the Pregnancy Discrimination Act of 1979, encoded as § 701(k) in Title VII, discrimination on the basis of pregnancy, childbirth, or related medical conditions is considered discrimination because of sex. Women affected by pregnancy and/or childbirth must be treated the same for all employment-related purposes, including fringe benefits such as health.

       1)   ***Abortion exception***—Employers are not compelled to pay for abortions under this provision.

    ii.   ***The Bennett Amendment***—Aimed at reconciling Title VII and the Equal Pay Act (discussed *infra* at V.E), the Bennett Amendment provides that a gender-based difference in pay will not violate Title VII if it is authorized by the Equal Pay Act.

    iii.   ***Sexual harassment*** is included in Title VII's protection of workers against discrimination "because of" sex. (See *Faragher* at V.C.2.iv.1.c *supra.*)

    iv.   ***Sexual orientation***—Discrimination on the basis of sexual orientation has been held not to violate Title VII's prohibition on discrimination because of sex.

c.   ***National Origin***—

    i.   Title VII protects both **citizens and non-citizens** from discrimination based on national origin. It is, however, permissible to discriminate based on U.S. citizenship status, so long as such discrimination is not a pretext or subterfuge for discrimination against persons based on national origin. Title VII requires that naturalized citizens and citizens born in the United States must be treated equally in employment.

    ii.   National-origin discrimination is also covered by **§ 1981** (discussed *infra* at V.D).

d.   ***Religion***—

    i.   Religious discrimination may be actionable under **all three models**: disparate treatment, disparate impact, and reasonable accommodation.

    ii.   **Reasonable accommodation** for religious beliefs under Title VII is much narrower than it is for disability status under the ADA.

1) ***The* TWA v. Hardison *Case:*** The Supreme Court held that it was permissible under Title VII for TWA to fire an employee for refusing to work on Saturday, which was his observed Sabbath day. TWA and the labor union could have changed the seniority system to give Sabbath observers preference in not working on Saturdays, or TWA could have left the seniority system in place but paid flight attendants overtime for Saturday work. The Court held, however, that Title VII did not require TWA to do either of these, because anything requiring more than a "de minimus" cost to the employer was not required as a "reasonable accommodation." *Trans World Airlines v. Hardison* (U.S. 1977).

iii. ***Relation to Unemployment Benefits***—Even where Title VII does not protect workers from discharge because of religious observances, the Free Exercise Clause of the First Amendment prohibits states from denying unemployment benefits to such workers. *Frazee v. Illinois Dep't of Employment Security* (U.S. 1989)

iv. ***Non-Belief***—Some courts hold that Title VII protects persons from discrimination based on their non-belief in any religion.

5. **Remedies**—Originally, Title VII only provided for remedies in equity, including an order to hire, reinstate, to disburse backpay, or in some cases to order the institution of affirmative action programs or education of employees about Title VII requirements. The Civil Rights Act of 1991 created 42 U.S.C. § 1981A, which allows compensatory and punitive damages for *intentional* discrimination under Title VII. Cases brought only under a theory of disparate impact will not be eligible for compensatory or punitive damages. Compensatories can include pain and suffering, mental anguish, inconvenience, and projected future pecuniary losses, but compensatory and punitive damages under Title VII are limited by statutory caps that are based on the size of the employer.

6. **Procedural Requirements / EEOC Enforcement**—Before suing under Title VII, plaintiffs must first exhaust any state administrative procedures and then exhaust all federal administrative procedures with the Equal Employment Opportunity Commission (EEOC). Federal courts have non-exclusive jurisdiction over Title VII suits, so state courts may hear them as well. Because the Civil Rights Act of 1991 added compensatory and punitive damages, plaintiffs are now entitled to a jury trial. Previously, with only equitable remedies available, all trials were conducted with the judge as factfinder.

D. Section 1981

1. **History**—The law at 42 U.S.C. § 1981 was passed in 1866 after the enactment of the 13th Amendment abolishing slavery. Although the statute overlaps significantly with Title VII, it is different in many respects.

2. **Prohibited Conduct**—Section 1981 prohibits racial discrimination in the making and enforcing of contracts. The language "[a]ll persons ... shall have the same right ... to make and enforce contracts ... as is enjoyed by white citizens" has been broadly interpreted as prohibiting discrimination based on race, ancestry, or ethnic characteristics, but not discrimination based on gender or religious (without ethnic) differences.

3. **Establishing a Violation**—The statute only works against intentional discrimination where the plaintiff can prove the defendant was motivated by race. According to *McDonald v. Santa Fe Trail Transportation Co.* (U.S. 1976), the statute implicates reverse discrimination against the majority white racial group as well as invidious discrimination against minority racial groups. Private actors as well as state and local government actors can be sued under § 1981.

4. **Remedies**—Plaintiffs may seek compensatory and punitive damages without limitation.

5. **Relation to Title VII**—Plaintiffs may sue under both Title VII and § 1981 if they are both applicable, but double recovery is not allowed.

   a. Section 1981 is *more comprehensive* than Title VII in several ways:

      i. There is no 15-employee minimum for coverage.

      ii. There are no statutory caps on damages.

      iii. Independent contractors are covered.

      iv. The statute goes beyond the employment context, creating equal rights in contract, property, and other contexts.

      v. There is no built-in statute of limitations, leaving the timeliness of the complaint to a determination of the applicable state statute of limitations.

      vi. There are no requirements of exhausting administrative avenues, as there is with Title VII.

   b. Section 1981 is *narrower* than Title VII in important ways:

      i. The statute only prohibits discrimination based on race, although "race" is broadly construed and includes "ethnicity," which overlaps significantly with national origin.

      ii. The statute only prohibits **intentional discrimination**. Theories of disparate impact are not available under § 1981.

E. Equal Pay Act

1. **Overview**—The Equal Pay Act (FLSA § 206(d)) is part of the Fair Labor Standards Act and predates the enactment of Title VII.

2. **Coverage**—The employer/employee coverage of the EPA is exactly the same as for the rest of the FLSA (see Chapter VI) with one important exception: There is no

"white-collar" exemption for executive, administrative, or professional employees as there is in regard to the minimum wage and overtime provisions of the FLSA. Unlike the broad anti-discrimination provisions of Title VII, the EPA only covers differences in compensation based on sex.

3. **Prima Facie Case for a Violation**—Four elements are required for a prima facie case under the EPA: (i) unequal pay, (ii) on the basis of sex, for (iii) equal work, in the (iv) same establishment.

   a. *Unequal Pay*

      i. The statute looks at the **rate of pay, not the net income** received by workers. Thus, a company violates this prong of the EPA if it pays a higher rate of commission to men in order to equalize income with women who have a higher sales volume because of prevailing market conditions.

      ii. Fringe benefits are considered "pay" for the purposes of the EPA.

   b. *On the Basis of Sex*

      i. For the prima facie case, the plaintiff only needs to show a pay differential between the sexes. The requirement is met if the plaintiff shows only that one person of the opposite sex is receiving a higher rate of pay than he or she is. There is **no prima facie requirement that sex actually motivated the pay differential**.

      ii. While the requirements for the prima facie case on this prong are often not difficult to meet, the employer may raise the **affirmative defense** that the pay differential is because of a factor other than sex. (See affirmative defenses *infra* at V.E.4.)

   c. *Equal Work*

      i. The jobs being compared need not be exactly the same, but they must be **"substantially equal."** The "equal work" inquiry is fact intensive. The jobs must have substantial equality of actual job duties.

      ii. The statutory standard for equal work is that the jobs being compared require "equal skill, effort, and responsibility and which are performed under similar working conditions." Thus, the focus is **what the jobs require, not what the job title is or what the individual skills are** of the individual workers in the two jobs. Individual skill or training differences might, however, be relevant to an affirmative defense that the differential is based on something "other than sex."

   d. *Same Establishment*—While "establishment" generally means the same place of business, the requirement has been broadly construed. For instance, two jobs of two teachers in the same school district can be compared even if they are in physically separate schools.

4. Affirmative Defenses

a. *Factors Other Than Sex*—The EPA allows employers to avoid a violation by showing that the pay differential was "pursuant to (i) a seniority system; (ii) a merit system; (iii) a system which measures earnings by quantity or quality of production, or (iv) a differential based on any other fact other than sex."

5. The Bennett Amendment—The Bennett Amendment is a provision of Title VII aimed at reconciling Title VII's prohibitions on sex-based discrimination with the EPA's provisions. Under the Bennett Amendment, **Title VII does not allow a cause of action for discrepancies in pay that are authorized by the EPA.**

6. Remedies and Enforcement—The EEOC or private parties can sue under the EPA. Because the EPA is a part of the FLSA and not Title VII, there is no requirement for plaintiffs to exhaust Title VII administrative procedures. Plaintiffs may recover backpay plus an equal amount as liquidated damages. The government, as a plaintiff, may seek injunctive relief.

F. Rehabilitation Act

1. Overview—The federal Rehabilitation Act (29 U.S.C. § 791 et. seq.), was passed in 1973 and amended substantially in 1978. The act was a groundbreaking statute providing broad protection against discrimination on the basis of disability, although **only with regard to a narrow category of employers with ties to the federal government**.

2. Protected Status: "Handicapped Individual"—The act protects a "handicapped individual," meaning a person who "has **a physical or mental impairment which substantially limits one or more of such person's major life activities**." The definition includes such things as loss of limbs, cosmetic disfigurement, mental retardation, and learning disabilities, but does not include conditions deemed to have cultural, economic, or environmental causes such as criminality and homosexuality. The definition of "disability" under the Rehabilitation Act is the same as the definition under the Americans with Disabilities Act. (See the discussion of the ADA, *infra* at V.G, for a more detailed explanation.)

3. Section 501: Federal Employers—All departments, agencies and "executive instrumentalities" of the federal government are **broadly prohibited from discriminating against employees on the basis of handicap**. Additionally, federal employers **must make reasonable accommodation and take affirmative action** in the hiring and promotion of disabled persons. Enforcement responsibilities lie with the EEOC.

4. Section 503: Federal Contractors—Federal contracts worth more than $10,000 must carry provisions which contractually bind the contractor **not to discriminate against disabled persons and to institute affirmative action in hiring and promoting "qualified" individuals with disabilities**. Qualified individuals are those that can perform the essential functions of the job with reasonable accommodation,

meaning accommodation that does not cause undue hardship for the employer. The Office of Federal Contract Compliance Programs enforces the provisions of § 503.

5. **Section 504: Federal Fund Recipients**—Qualified disabled persons **cannot be discriminated against in any program or activity funded by the federal government**. This section covers many hospitals, school districts, universities, transit authorities, and other federally assisted bodies. As with § 503, "qualified" individuals are those that can perform the essential functions of the job with reasonable accommodation short of undue hardship on the employer. Unlike other sections of the Rehabilitation Act, § 504 creates a private right of action for plaintiffs who have been discriminated against.

G. Americans with Disabilities Act

1. **Overview**—Modeled on Title VII of the Civil Rights Act of 1964 and the Rehabilitation Act, the Americans with Disabilities Act was enacted in 1990. The ADA has five titles. Two titles are important in the employment context. Title I specifically deals with employment discrimination, and Title V's list of miscellaneous provisions both enlarge and restrict the operation of Title I. The ADA is the only *comprehensive* federal scheme for prohibiting discrimination against those with mental and physical disabilities. The most important areas of case-law development have been through interpreting the meanings of "disability" and "reasonable accommodation."

2. **Coverage**—The ADA applies to employers affecting commerce who have 15 or more employees.

3. **Prohibited Discrimination**—Section 102 provides that no covered entity shall discriminate against a **qualified individual with a disability** because of the disability of such individual with regard to job applications, hiring, advancement, discharge, compensation, training, or other terms, conditions, and privileges of employment. The statute specifically enumerates several factual situations as examples of prohibited discrimination:

   - Engaging in a contractual relationship that imposes prohibited discrimination;
   - Utilizing standards that:
     —have the effect of discrimination, or
     —perpetuate the discrimination of others subject to administrative control;
   - Not making reasonable accommodation;
   - Intentionally screening out through facially neutral criteria;
   - Conducting discriminatory medical examinations or obtaining or disseminating medical information (with some exceptions).

4. **Protected Class—"Qualified Individual with a Disability"**

a. ***Definition of "Disability"***—There are **three alternative definitions** under which an individual can claim the ADA's protection.

    i.   A physical or mental impairment that substantially limits one or more major life activities;

    ii.   A record of such impairment;

    iii.   Being regarded as having such an impairment.

Notice that because of the second and third definitions, if an employer wrongfully discriminates against an individual it believes to be disabled, the employer cannot escape liability by claiming that the individual does not, in fact, have such an impairment.

b. ***Three-Prong Test***—For the first definition of "disability," the Act's definition is often restated as a three-prong test:

    i.   A physical or mental impairment;

    ii.   That substantially limits;

    iii.   One or more major life activities.

c. ***Definition of "Impairment"***—An "impairment" is a mental or physical disorder that is outside the normal range. The EEOC guidelines provide that, for instance, having green eyes or left-handedness is not an impairment, even if it precludes employment.

d. ***Definition of "Substantially Limit"***—The "substantially limit" prong prevents broken bones or other temporary impairments from being covered under the ADA.

e. ***Definition of "Major Life Activities"***—Working at a particular job, by itself, is not a "major life activity," although working at a broad range of jobs is a major life activity. Thus if an impairment keeps an individual from working at a particular job, but not most other jobs within that same activity, then the impairment does not qualify as a disability.

    i.   ***Example:*** Florence, a legal secretary, is allergic to the fabric used to cover the cubicle walls in the offices of the law firm Weston & Harley, but she is not allergic to office interiors in general. Florence does not have a disability, because working at Weston & Harley is not a major life activity. If Florence were allergic to all synthetic fabrics, however, she would have a disability. Florence's claim against Weston & Harley can also be disposed of based on the definition of "substantially limit." While working in a law firm might be a "major life activity," not being able to work for one specific law firm would not be viewed as "substantially limiting" one's ability to work in law firms in general.

f. ***Specific Exclusions from "Disability"***—The ADA specifically provides that certain statuses or conditions are not "disabilities" under the Act:

i. Homosexuality or bisexuality;

ii. Transvestitism, transexualism, pedophilia, exhibitionism, voyeurism, gender identity disorders not resulting from physical impairments, or other sexual behavior disorders;

iii. Compulsive gambling, kleptomania, or pyromania;

iv. Psychoactive substance-use disorders resulting from current illegal use of drugs.

    1) Note that disabilities incurred from past illegal use of drugs are not excluded.

g. ***Definition of "Qualified Individual"***—"Qualified individual with a disability" means a person who, with or without reasonable accommodation, can perform the essential functions of the employment position that he or she desires or holds. Consideration is given to the employer's statement of required job functions.

5. **Reasonable Accommodation**—Reasonable accommodation means taking affirmative steps to alter the workplace or job duties so that a disabled person may work.

a. ***Examples***—"Reasonable accommodation" may include: making physical facilities accessible, restructuring schedules, reassigning, acquiring equipment, adjusting examinations, providing training materials or policies, providing readers or interpreters, or making other accommodations.

b. ***Limits of Reasonability Under* Vande Zande**—According to Judge Posner in *Vande Zande v. State of Wisconsin Department of Administration* (7th Cir. 1995), the employee must show that the accommodation is reasonable in the sense that it is both efficacious and proportional to the costs incurred. Once this prime facie burden is met, the defendant can prove that a more careful consideration of the costs shows that it is excessive in relation to the benefits of the accommodation. Employers do not have to spend even minimal amounts of money to bring working conditions for disabled and non-disabled employees into absolute identity.

c. ***Duty to Assist***—Employers have a duty to explore accommodations, and disabled individuals have a complimentary duty to assist in this exploration.

d. ***Employee Preference Does Not Control***—The employee's preference for accommodation has little to do with what is required. Employers are not required to provide the specific accommodation requested by the employee if some other accommodation will suffice. Likewise, merely satisfying the employee's preference may not be enough.

e. ***Relation to "Undue Hardship"***—"Reasonable" is a separate limit from "undue hardship." For instance, even if an accommodation would not cause any hardship to the employer—since the accommodation might be minimal in cost and the employer might have vast resources—the employer is still not obligated to provide the accommodation if it is unreasonable.

i. ***The* Vande Zande *Case:*** Vande Zande sued her employer, the State of Wisconsin, to have the office kitchen's sink lowered two inches. The state agency had a sink in the restroom that was of a suitable height for her use already. Because Vande Zande already had access to a usable sink, further accommodation would be unreasonable. *Vande Zande v. State of Wisconsin Department of Administration* (7th Cir. 1995).

6. **Defenses—**

   a. ***Business Necessity***—Some qualifications for a job may be permitted even if they cause the job to be denied to certain disabled persons, if the qualification is job related, consistent with a business necessity, and there is no reasonable accommodation that will allow performance of the job.

   b. ***Direct Threat to Health or Safety***—Where accommodation would pose a direct threat to the health or safety of other individuals in the workplace, the employer has not violated the ADA.

   c. ***Undue Hardship***—When accommodation would impose an undue hardship on the employer, there is no violation. "Undue hardship" means that an accommodation requires significant difficulty or expense. Relevant to finding whether an accommodation would cause an undue hardship are:

      i. The nature and cost of the accommodation;

      ii. The financial resources of the facility and the impact on the operation of the facility;

      iii. The overall financial resources of the employer and its size, type, and location of its facilities;

      iv. The geographic separateness, administrative, or fiscal relationship of facilities with regard to the covered entity.

   d. There are various exceptions for food handling.

7. **Relation to Benefit Plans and Insurance**—ADA § 501(c) specifically exempts several practices related to benefit plans and insurance. The section says that the ADA shall not prohibit or restrict:

   a. Insurers or health care entities from classifying individuals on the basis or risk;

   b. Employers from establishing a benefit plan based on underwriting risks;

   c. A person or organization covered by the Act from establishing, sponsoring, observing or administering the terms of a bona fide benefit plan that is not subject to state laws that regulate insurance.

8. **Remedies / Enforcement**—The ADA incorporates Title VII remedies, including back pay, reinstatement, court-ordered accommodations, and compensatory and punitive damages.

9. **Whistleblower / Anti-retaliation Provision**—Discrimination on the basis of one's assertion of rights under the ADA is prohibited. Coercion, intimidation, or other

interference with an individual's enjoyment of a right under the ADA is likewise prohibited. The ADA's regular remedies are available to persons coerced or discriminated against because of their assertion of rights.

H. Age Discrimination in Employment Act

1. **Overview**—The Age Discrimination in Employment Act of 1967 (ADEA) works much like Title VII, but with the protected status being age. Unlike Title VII, however, there is a limited protected class: Only persons 40-years or older are protected. Also, the ADEA has more exceptions, in the form of affirmative defenses, and therefore acknowledges a broader range of permissible discrimination than Title VII does.

2. **Coverage**—Only employers in an industry affecting commerce who have 20 or more employees are covered by the ADEA. As amended, the ADEA applies to public employers, although there are exceptions for fire fighters and police officers.

3. **Protected Class**—The ADEA only creates a cause of action for persons **over the age of 40**. Section 4 of the act prohibits discrimination "because of age." Section 12 of the act, entitled "Limits," provides that only plaintiffs over the age of 40 will have a cause of action under the act.

    a. *Anti-Younger Discrimination*—Whether or not anti-younger discrimination is prohibited by the ADEA is an unsettled matter of law. Commentators disagree on the issue.

        i. *Statutory language*—Although it seems odd, according the statutory language, it does not matter whether the discrimination is against younger persons and in favor of older persons, or against older persons in favor of younger persons. So long as the discrimination is against persons over the age of 40, it is prohibited.

        ii. *Case law and congressional findings*—Despite the broad statutory language, the cases interpreting the ADEA and the congressional findings of fact generally suppose that the ADEA's purpose is to prohibit discrimination against older workers in favor of younger workers, not the other way around. At least two circuit courts have ruled that the ADEA does not allow a cause of action for anti-younger discrimination.

    b. *Executive/Policymaker Exemption*—While covered by the Act generally, employees who are in bona fide executive or high-level policymaking positions may be mandatorily retired at age 65 if they are entitled to at least $44,000 in annual retirement benefits.

4. **Establishing a Violation**—To establish a prima facie case for violation of the ADEA, the plaintiff may use either disparate treatment or disparate-impact theories.

    a. *Disparate Treatment*

        i. *Prima facie case*—A plaintiff must show that he or she:

1) Is over 40 years old;

2) Suffered an adverse action, such as discharge or rejection of employment application;

3) Was qualified for the position;

4) Was replaced or passed up for a worker who is under 40 or significantly younger.

Note that these requirements may be rephrased according to what kind of action is being challenged.

ii. *Defendant's burden of production*—After a prima facie case is established, the defendant then only has a burden of producing a legitimate, nondiscriminatory reason for the adverse employment action. Alternatively, the defendant may assert an affirmative defense.

iii. *Plaintiff's burden of proof*—After the defense has produced a nondiscriminatory reason, the plaintiff may prevail by showing that the reason was a pretext.

iv. *Mixed-motive cases*—Where age was one of multiple reasons for the adverse employment decision, the plaintiff will prevail if age discrimination was a but-for cause of the employment action. If the defendant can show that the result would have been the same regardless of the consideration of age, then the defendant will prevail.

b. *Disparate Impact*—The disparate-impact theory is also available in ADEA cases. Because increased age tends to correlate with higher salaries, employers often find it advantageous to target layoffs to higher-salaried workers, and in such situations older workers are often disproportionately affected. The ADEA exempts decisions made on "reasonable factors other than age," but the law is not settled on whether this includes salary-based decisions attacked under a disparate-impact analysis.

5. **Affirmative Defenses**—The ADEA allows important affirmative defenses:

a. *Bona-Fide Occupational Qualification*—As with Title VII, the ADEA allows a BFOQ defense. In *Western Air Lines, Inc. v. Criswell* (U.S. 1985), Criswell challenged Western Air Lines' rule against employing flight engineers over age 60, which the airline defended as a BFOQ. The Court held that the BFOQ defense for the ADEA is applied the same way as for Title VII.

i. *The* **Tamiami** *Test*—The test for the BFOQ as set forth in *Usery v. Tamiami Trail Tours, Inc.* (5th Cir. 1976), and recited by the Supreme Court in *Western Air Lines, Inc. v. Criswell* (U.S. 1985), is:

1) *Peripheral nature*—Some qualifications can be so peripheral to the central mission of the employer's business that no discrimination can be "reasonably necessary to the normal operation of the particular business."

2) ***Reasonably necessary to the particular business***—The qualifications must be more than "convenient" or "reasonable"; they must be "reasonably necessary ... to the particular business." And the employer must be compelled to use age (or another qualification) as a proxy for the job-related qualification validated in the first inquiry. This can be done in two ways.

a) The employer had reasonable cause to believe that substantially all of the persons outside the qualification would be unable to perform safely and efficiently the duties of the job, ***or***

b) The employer can establish that age is a legitimate proxy for the job qualification by proving that it is "impossible or highly impractical" to deal with the older employees on an individualized basis.

b. ***Bona-Fide Employee Benefit Plans***—For some benefits, such as life insurance, the cost to the employer for providing the benefit increases as the employee gets older. Because of this, the ADEA, as amended by the **Older Workers Benefit Protection Act of 1990** (OWBPA), allows employers to offer different benefits to employees based on age, so long as they are spending the same amount or more to provide the more limited benefits to older people as they spend to provide benefits for younger people. Additionally, the claimed bona-fide employee benefit plan cannot be a subterfuge to evade the purposes of the act. That is, if the employer has structured the benefit plan in such a way as to weed out older workers, the affirmative defense will fail.

i. ***Early retirement programs***—Under *Karlen v. City of College of Chicago* (9th Cir. 1988) and the OWBPA, voluntary early retirement programs are permissible as long as they are truly voluntary and only offer incentives to retire, rather than adverse consequences for not retiring.

c. ***Bona-Fide Seniority Systems***—Seniority systems are allowed so long as they are truly based on seniority, and not on age.

6. **Remedies and Enforcement**—The ADEA generally incorporates the remedies of the FLSA, with some modifications. The EEOC has the right to investigate and litigate ADEA matters, and there is an administrative exhaustion requirement. Private plaintiffs have a cause of action and may recover back pay plus, where the violation was willful, an equal amount as liquidated damages. Compensatory and punitive damages are not available. Injunctive relief is available both for the government and for private plaintiffs.

I. Sexual Orientation

1. **No Applicable Federal Law**—There is no federal legislation that protects employees from discrimination based on their sexual orientation. It is well established that Title

VII does not protect against sexual-orientation discrimination as discrimination that is "because of" sex.

2. **State and Local Laws**—Gays and lesbians are increasingly protected by state and local laws and ordinances of varying kinds. California law, for instance, prohibits discrimination on the basis of sexual orientation for all employers with five or more employees. *California Labor Code § 1102.1.*

J. State Laws

1. **Overview**—State laws often add to federal protections in important ways, such as by extending the coverage, scope, or remedies available for a certain kind of discrimination. Whenever plaintiffs find that a federal statute does not allow them a cause of action because of some limitation, by turning to state law they may find a broader anti-discrimination scheme that will allow them recovery.

2. **Small Employers**—While federal statutes such as Title VII and the EPA exempt employers with less than a certain number of employees, state statutes often extend the same substantive protection to smaller workplaces.

3. **Procedural Issues**—Requirements of administrative exhaustion, statutes of limitations, damages caps, burdens of proof and other procedural issues might also be viewed differently under state law so as to create advantages for plaintiffs above and beyond federal law.

4. **Preclusion in Anti-Discrimination Compared to Other Areas of Employment Law**—While other federal statutory schemes in employment law, such as ERISA and OSHA, have severe preclusive effects on the ability of states to create causes of actions for employees, federal anti-discrimination law generally allows as much additional state lawmaking as the states desire, so long as the states are expanding protection for workers, rather than restricting protection.

K. Constitutional Rights for Public Employees

Because most employment law classes do not discuss constitutional law as applied to public employment discrimination, and because most constitutional law classes do, no lengthy discussion is provided in this outline.

1. **General**—While federal discrimination statutes cover most public employees for most types of discrimination, public employees may additionally assert rights under the Equal Protection Clause of the U.S. Constitution.

2. **Section 1983**—The law at 42 U.S.C. § 1983, passed in 1871, allows a cause of action for the violation of constitutional rights. The statute prohibits persons acting "under color of" state law to deprive a person of "any rights, privileges, or immunities secured by the Constitution and laws." The statute thus allows public employees to

sue at law or in equity for discrimination in the workplace as a denial of equal protection. Note that § 1983 has no impact on private employees and employers.

3. **No Disparate-Impact Analysis**—One important difference in the interpretation of discrimination statutes and the Constitution is that under *Washington v. Davis* (U.S. 1976), disparate-impact analysis cannot be used to establish constitutional violations.

CHAPTER VI

WAGES AND HOURS

For the Equal Pay Act, please see V.E.

A. History

1. **Wage Abuses**—At and before the turn of the century, employers imposed a number of conditions on the wages and hours of their employees that were viewed as abusive. Some employers would pay employees only in script—non-cash coupons—which could only be exchanged for merchandise in an employer-owned store. Other employers would require extremely long hours of their employees, creating stress for workers and their families.

2. *Lochner* **and the Invalidity of State Law**—In the late 1800's, states enacted laws to regulate wages and hours. But the famous case of *Lochner v. New York* (U.S. 1905) and its progeny declared much of this legislation unconstitutional. In *Lochner*, a law limited the number of hours bakers could work. The Court struck down the law as an unconstitutional restriction on the freedom of contract, a right found in the original unamended Constitution. Minimum wage laws and federal-labor-standards laws were among the casualties of *Lochner* jurisprudence.

3. **The End of the** *Lochner* **Era and the FLSA**—In the midst of the Great Depression, the Supreme Court reversed its position and upheld the constitutionality of a state minimum-wage law in *West Coast Hotel Co. v. Parrish* (U.S. 1937). Congress soon followed up with the Federal Labor Standards Act of 1938, which, among other things, set a minimum wage, restricted hours, and prohibited child labor. The constitutionality of the FLSA was upheld in 1940. The FLSA was originally intended not only to protect workers, but also to lift the country out of the Great Depression by increasing the purchasing power of workers, thus revitalizing the economy. Since the end of the Depression, the policy focus has been on protecting workers.

B. Theory

1. **Economic Arguments Against the Minimum Wage**—Many commentators argue that the minimum wage is harmful because it restricts the free market for labor, and thus prevents the market from reaching the most efficient allocation of capital. They argue that raising wages through a minimum wage will squeeze employers, and employers will not be able to afford as many workers, leading to increased unemployment. If firms do not immediately lay off workers, these commentators argue, they will need to raise prices to compensate for the higher wages, which will lead to a decrease in sales, and thus lead to laying off workers eventually.

a. ***Critique of Economic Arguments Against the Minimum Wage***

    i.   ***Falling employer profits***—Commentators opposed to the minimum wage often fail to consider decreasing corporate profits as a third variable in the economic equation. While this might cause investors to pull their capital out of the affected company, if the entire economy is impacted by a slight loss in profits because of the minimum wage, then the result will be a net transfer of wealth from capital owners to lower-income workers.

    ii.   ***Real-world variables***—While those opposed to the minimum wage cite economic theory, proponents of the minimum wage point out reasons why the theory is not directly applicable to the real world. Economic models, such as the ones used by minimum-wage opponents, assume that all parties will have perfect information, job mobility, and equal bargaining power. Proponents point out that employers often have a much stronger bargaining position than workers do, especially those who are the lowest paid. They further point out that many workers have limited information about the labor market and are tied to jobs because of family or community considerations, which prevent those workers from being mobile.

    iii.   ***The benefits of lost jobs in a global economy***—In a global economy, if the minimum wage is high enough, some industries—such as clothing and shoe manufacturing—may move operations overseas. Some commentators argue that this is good because it causes first-world countries to retrain their labor force for higher-skill, higher-paying jobs and allows third-world countries the economic boost of increased manufacturing jobs.

2. **Economic Arguments Against Other Labor Standards**—Commentators may use economic models to argue against other labor standards, such as overtime pay, hour restrictions, and prohibitions on child labor. They argue, as with the minimum wage, that such standards interfere with the free market, and thus lead to an inefficient outcome.

    a.   ***Critique of Economic Arguments Against Other Labor Standards***—Proponents of other labor standards may critique the economic arguments by attacking their assumptions about bargaining power, job mobility, and perfect information (as with the minimum wage, *supra* at VI.B.1.a). Additionally, proponents argue that overtime restrictions force firms to hire more workers, reducing the unemployment rate. Proponents may, however, simply reject economic arguments altogether, arguing instead that the quality-of-life issues involved in labor standards—such as allowing workers to spend time with their families, and preventing children from growing up too quickly—are more important than any economic efficiency that might result from the repeal of such standards.

C. The Fair Labor Standards Act (FLSA)

1. **Overview**—The substantive provisions of the FLSA include the minimum wage, mandated overtime pay, and child-labor restrictions. While applying the substantive provisions can occasionally be problematic, one of the most frequently litigated aspects of the FLSA is the extent of its coverage—that is, whether a worker is covered by the provisions of the FLSA.

2. **Coverage**—There are many limitations on the coverage of the FLSA. Exceptions that apply only to one portion of the FLSA are covered under the discussion of that portion. The following are general limitations.

   a. *Interstate Commerce Requirement*—The FLSA only applies to enterprises and workers engaged in interstate commerce. The broad interpretation of interstate commerce means that almost all businesses are covered. An exception might be very small local businesses where the only employee is a spouse or child of the owner.

   b. *Only Employees Are Covered*—Only "employees" are covered by the FLSA. (See I.B *supra*.)

   c. *Specific Industries Exempted*—Because of separate federal regulatory schemes for certain industries, the FLSA exempts railroads, airlines, and other businesses.

   d. *White-Collar Exemptions*— The FLSA exempts professional, administrative, and executive workers and outside sales persons from the overtime and wage provisions.

      i. To qualify for the exemption for professional, administrative, and executive workers, the employer must meet both a "salary test" and a "duties test."

         1) *Salary test*—The employee must get a "salary," which is compensation paid at regular intervals regardless of how many hours are worked. Several courts have held that if the employer can dock salary pay for a person's failure to work eight hours in a day, then the salary test is not met. Courts are split on whether supplemental overtime pay is evidence of non-salary pay.

         2) *Duties test*—An analysis of the duties of the employee will determine whether the employee can be considered "professional," "administrative," or "executive." *FLSA § 213(a)(1), Dalheim v. KDFW-TV* (5th Cir. 1990).

            a) *Executive*—To count as "executive," the employee's "primary duty" must be the "management of the enterprise." The definition of "primary duty" is not simply a function of the amount of time spent on such activities, but "over 50 percent" of the time being spent on managerial tasks militates in favor of finding executive status. An employee who does not supervise or manage other employees cannot be considered an executive.

    b)   *Professional*—To count as "professional," the employee must have minimal supervision and a wide degree of latitude to use creativity and independent thinking in determining how to complete assigned tasks.

    c)   *Administrative*—The standards for the administrative exemption require that the job involve (i) office or nonmanual work, (ii) that is directly related to management policies or general business operations, and (iii) involves the exercise of discretion and independent judgment.

3. Minimum Wage—Workers must not be paid less than a certain wage per hour, as established by federal law. The minimum wage at the beginning of 2000 was $5.15. *FLSA § 206.* Congress amends the FLSA to revise the amount from time to time.

  a. *Exceptions:*

    i.   *Piece rates and wages by periods other than hours*—Wages paid as piece rates are permissible. For example, an employer may pay $1 per basket of strawberries picked. Alternatively, employers may set compensation as so much per week, month, or year. Regardless of the compensation system, however, **workers must actually receive the minimum wage per hour worked**.

    ii.   *Room and board*—Employers can deduct money for the actual cost of board and lodging, allowing the amount actually disbursed to the employee to fall below the minimum wage.

    iii.   *Tips*—The employer can credit tips against the minimum wage, as long as the tips were actually received by the employee. Regardless of how much the employee receives in tips, however, the employer must directly pay at least a certain minimum amount to the employee. In the beginning of 2000, this amount was $2.13. If $2.13 plus the amount of the tips falls blow the minimum wage, then the employer must make up the difference.

       1)   The $2.13 rule replaces an older rule that required employer-paid cash to equal one-half the minimum wage.

    iv.   *Employer/employee coverage*—Where either the employer or the employee is not covered by the FLSA, the minimum-wage provisions will not apply.

    v.   *Disabled subminimum wage*—Subminimum wages can be paid to some substantially disabled workers, such as retarded persons working in a non-profit, sheltered workshop facility.

    vi.   *Youth-training subminimum wage*—A subminimum youth-training wage is permitted during the first 90 days of employment for a worker 19-years-old or younger. At the beginning of 2000, the probationary wage was $4.25.

    1)   Employers are **prohibited from displacing regular workers** with workers earning the subminimum youth-training wage.

4. Overtime Pay

a. ***1.5 Times Regular Wage***—If an employee works over 40 hours in a week, these additional hours are called "overtime." Employees must be paid 1.5 times their regular wage for the overtime hours. *FLSA § 207(a)(1).*

    i.   ***Benefits are not wages***—Fringe benefits cannot offset overtime pay. This includes insurance benefits and paid vacation time. The employer must pay 1.5 times the base rate. *Dunlop v. Gray-Goto, Inc.* (10th Cir. 1976).

    ii.   ***Compensatory time off for public employers***—Public employers can give compensatory time off in lieu of overtime pay, provided that employees do not accumulate more than 240 hours of such time, and that they are able to take the time off whenever they want unless it would cause a significant disruption.

b. ***Industry-Specific Exemptions***—Different overtime rules apply to hospital workers, police, fire fighters, and other workers in industries with an unusual need for unorthodox scheduling.

c. ***Determining the Number of Hours***—One of the most important problems of interpreting the overtime provisions of the FLSA is the calculation of how many hours are worked in a week.

    i.   ***On-call time***—Time that employees must make themselves available to work on short notice, known as "on-call time," **may or may not be counted** toward overtime. The more restrictive the on-call conditions are, and the fewer personal activities that may be pursued during the on-call time, the more likely it is that a court will find that the on-call time is compensable.

        1)   **The *Bright* Case:** In *Bright v. Houston Northwest Medical Center Survivor, Inc.* (5th Cir. 1992), a repair technician was never allowed to be intoxicated or to roam more than 20 minutes away from the hospital for which he worked. These restrictions applied even during his vacations. The court held that the on-call time was not compensable, because the hours could be used for his own purposes, despite the restrictions on his freedom.

        2)   **The *Renfro* Case:** In *Renfro v. City of Emporia* (10th Cir. 1991), a municipal government was required to pay damages to fire fighters for on-call time, even though some of them used those hours to work second jobs. The court held that the frequency of the callbacks—three-to-five times a day—made the on-call time so burdensome that it was compensable.

ii. **_Waiting time_**—Generally, waiting time at or near the workplace is compensable unless the time is long enough and permissive enough that employees can use the time for their own benefit.

iii. **_Breaks_**—Breaks of less than 20 minutes are compensable, but longer breaks are not compensable if workers are not engaged in work-related activities.

iv. **_Travel time_**—Time spent commuting from home to work is not compensable, but once the workday has begun, time spent traveling between jobsites is usually compensable.

5. **Child Labor**—The FLSA prohibits "oppressive child labor," as defined both by the FLSA and through regulations of the Department of Labor. The minimum age for most jobs is 16. For hazardous jobs, 18 is the minimum age. Children aged 14 and 15 are permitted in certain jobs in sectors such as retail or food service, but there are several restrictions on their employment. The restrictions include the provision that they may not work for more than eight hours a day, or for more than three hours on a school day. Even younger children are permitted to deliver newspapers or do some agricultural work, such as work for a parent on a family farm.

6. **Enforcement**—There are various provisions for claims of action under the FLSA.

   a. **_Section 216(a) Criminal Penalties_**—Criminal fines are authorized for violators, and imprisonment is authorized for repeat offenders.

   b. **_Section 216(b) Employee Civil Suit_**—Employees may sue for unpaid minimum wages or overtime pay plus an equal amount in liquidated damages. Victorious plaintiffs may also be awarded attorney's fees and reinstatement.

   c. **_Section 216(c) Government Civil Suit on Behalf of Employees_**— The Secretary of Labor may sue on behalf of employees for the recovery of unpaid minimum wages or overtime pay plus an equal amount in liquidated damages.

   d. **_Section 217 Civil Suit for Injunctive Relief_**—This section authorizes injunctions imposed by federal courts, and can be used to prohibit interstate shipment of goods manufactured in violation of the FLSA.

D. The Portal-to-Portal Act

The Portal-to-Portal Act of 1947 compliments the FLSA by clarifying what time constitutes compensable work time. Commuting time, i.e., traveling to and from work, is not compensable work time. But traveling from one jobsite to another, time spent traveling on errands for work, or time spent traveling when coming back to work from home because of a work-related emergency, *is* compensable work time. In addition, if travel constitutes a principal part of the job, then travel time may be compensable.

E. The Family and Medical Leave Act

1. **Overview**—The Family and Medical Leave Act of 1993 requires employers to grant unpaid leave to employees because of illness of the employee or of a family member, or because of childbirth or adoption.

2. **Coverage**—The FMLA applies only to employers with 50 or more employees. The employer-size requirement is larger than in other federal legislation because of a belief that larger employers will better be able to endure a prolonged period without any given employee. Only employees, as the FLSA defines them, who have worked over a 12-month period with at least 1,250 hours of service at the employer, are eligible for FMLA leave.

3. **Duration of Leave**—Employees may take up to 12 weeks of unpaid leave in any 12-month period. Employers may, however, require employees to take accrued vacation or sick days, or employer-provided family or medical leave as part of that 12-week period.

4. **Benefits During Leave**—The employer must continue to provide the same health benefits that the employee was entitled to during regular employment. If the employee does not come back from leave, however, the employer may obtain reimbursement of premiums from the employee.

5. **Reasons for Leave**—

   a. *Childbirth, Adoption, or Foster Care*—Employees may take leave at anytime within the first 12 months after the birth, adoption, or placement for foster care of a child.

   b. *Serious Health Condition*—Employees may take leave to take care of a child, spouse, or parent with a "serious health condition," or because of their own serious health condition. "Serious health condition" is defined as an illness, injury, impairment, or physical or mental condition involving inpatient or continuing care.

6. **Notice, Timing, and Certification Requirements**—

   a. *Notice*—When the leave is foreseeable, the employee must give the employer 30 days notice when possible.

   b. *Timing*—For a planned medical treatment that will result in foreseeable medical leave, the employee must make a reasonable effort to schedule the treatment so as not to unduly disrupt the employer's operations.

   c. *Certification*—The employer may require certification of the serious health condition for which leave is sought, and the employee must, in a timely manner, provide the certification to the employer. At the employer's expense, the employer may require a second opinion of a health care provider with regard to the health condition. If the first and second opinions do not agree, the employer may require a third opinion.

7. **Restoration After Leave**—Upon returning from leave, the employer must restore the employee to the same position, or to an equivalent position with the same benefits, pay, and other terms and conditions.

   a. *Highly Compensated Employees Exemption*—With notice, an employer may deny restoration to an employee who is among the highest-paid 10 percent of employees if the restoration would result in "substantial and grievous economic injury" to the employer's operations.

F. State Wage and Hour Regulation

1. **No Federal Preemption**—In contrast to ERISA's preemption of state benefit regulation, the states are free to enact their own regulation of wages and hours, and many states have.

2. **State Regulation May be Stricter**—The states may impose higher minimum wages, overtime rates, or may cover employers and workers that are not covered by the FLSA or FMLA.

CHAPTER VII

BENEFITS

A. Introduction

1. **Why Benefits?**—Fringe benefits, or simply "benefits," are ways of compensating an employee aside from paying cash wages. Benefits may include retirement plans, health insurance, life insurance, vacation days, child care, access to a gym, or various other non-cash items. Employers often prefer offering benefits rather than higher wages because:

   a. Employers receive favorable tax treatment under the Internal Revenue Code, and

   b. Group purchasing power allows employers to buy insurance, pension plans, gym membership, and other items for a lower cost than employees would pay individually.

   Thus, the overall benefit to the employee may be higher than it would be if companies merely paid the cost of benefits to the employees in the form of higher wages. Other benefits, such as vacation days and sick leave, cannot be purchased from outside vendors. Unless the employer offers time off as a benefit, employees will not receive it, and employees may feel that increased pay could not offset the loss to their quality of life that would occur if they were not allowed time off.

2. **History**—

   a. *The Failure of the Common Law*—Before the passage of state and federal legislation regulating benefits, employers often took advantage of employees with benefit plans. Many plans had loopholes for the employers, so while workers labored under the belief that they would receive a pension or other benefits, employers escaped the burden of paying for the benefits, and workers were deprived of the ability to retire or get medical treatment. Legally, these employers were aided by the **gratuity theory of pensions**, according to which pensions were simply gifts from the employer to the employee and not part of a contract. By classifying pensions as mere donative promises, courts refused to allow breach-of-contract suits to recover pension benefits on the theory that there was no consideration to support a binding contract.

   b. *Myriad State Regulatory Schemes*—In response to the failures of the common law to regulate benefits, states enacted various statutory schemes. The protection of these systems varied, and employers who had employees in multiple states found it very difficult to design uniform benefit plans that met the requirements of each state in which the employer was operating.

   c. *Federal ERISA Legislation*—Because of the difficulties interstate employers experienced in offering benefits, and because of continuing abuse by unscrupulous employers who took advantage of the lack of regulation in some states, Congress passed ERISA legislation (discussed *infra* at VII.C), which replaced all state regulation with a uniform federal scheme.

B. Typology of Benefits

1. **Pension Plans**—Pension plans provide cash payments to employees during their retirement. There are two broad categories of pension plans: defined benefit plans and defined contribution plans.

   a. ***Defined Benefit Plans***—Defined benefit plans distribute a set amount of money to retirees per unit of time. For instance, a defined benefit plan might provide for a cash benefit of $2,000 per month after retirement. Because the payments to beneficiaries are defined years in advance, employers must project how much money they will need to contribute in order for the pension fund to have the requisite amount available for beneficiaries in the future. In defined benefit plans, the employer assumes the investment risk and must contribute additional funds if the fund's investments do not perform. The employer may, however, keep any surplus monies if the investments perform better than expected.

   b. ***Defined Contribution Plans***—Defined contribution plans place the investment risk on the employees. Employers guarantee a set contribution of money per unit of time to the pension. Because the invested money may have varying rates of returns, the amount of money paid to employees at retirement can vary. For instance, a defined contribution plan might guarantee that $300 will be invested into the pension fund on behalf of each employee every month; the amount available to employees at retirement will depend on how the investments have performed in the meantime.

2. **Welfare Benefits**—So-called welfare benefits are non-cash benefits such as vacation days, sick days, paid leave, life insurance, health-club memberships and, most notably, health care and medical insurance.

C. ERISA

1. **Introduction**—The Employee Retirement Income Security Act of 1974 is an extraordinarily complex federal scheme that was enacted in response to the increasing importance of benefits as employee compensation and the increasing difficulty faced by interstate employers in implementing uniform pension plans that would satisfy the different regulatory schemes of multiple states.

   a. ***Does Not Require Establishment***—ERISA does not require the establishment of any benefit plans. The law only prescribes regulation for those employers who chose to offer such plans.

   b. ***Regulates Pensions Plans, But Not Welfare Benefits***—While ERISA provides very detailed substantive regulation of pension plans, the original act does not provide substantive regulation of welfare benefits, such as health care. Federal

COBRA and HIPAA legislation (discussed *infra* at VII.D) later added some isolated regulations for health-care benefits.

c. ***Broad Preemption***—ERISA is well known for having one of the broadest preemption clauses of any federal statute. Almost all state law regulating employee benefits is preempted, including any state regulation of welfare benefits.

d. ***Vacuum of Welfare-Benefit Regulation***—Since the unamended act does not regulate welfare benefits, yet precludes any state regulations, ERISA has left a vacuum of substantive regulation in this area. This alleged deficiency has been a point of considerable controversy, especially with regard to the lack of regulation over employee health plans.

2. **Title I: Substantive Pension Plan Regulation**—The provisions of ERISA for regulating pension plans, located in Title I, are enormously complex. They include requirements for periodic vesting, diversification of investments, the rate at which benefits accrue, detailed reporting to government agencies, and the dissemination of information to employees in a form comprehensible to the average plan beneficiary.

3. **Title IV: Plan Termination Insurance / The PBGC**—Title IV of ERISA created the Pension Benefit Guaranty Corporation (PBGC) to administer an insurance program for defined benefit plans so that employees may receive benefits even if their plan terminates. The provisions of Title IV have disincentivized employers from creating defined benefit plans, thus making defined contribution plans more desirable.

4. **ERISA and the Internal Revenue Code**—The Internal Revenue Code allows "qualified" pension plans to enjoy significant tax savings, and the code sets forth numerous standards that retirement plans have to meet before they will be tax-qualified. Most firms with pension plans follow the Code requirements so that they can receive the tax savings. While the standards for pension plans under ERISA and the Code overlap, the Code has more standards than ERISA.

a. ***Enforcement***—The Internal Revenue Code can only be enforced by the Internal Revenue Service. The penalty for pension plans that do not adhere to Code requirements is simply a loss of tax-qualified status. The revocation of such status, however, could constitute a substantial financial loss.

5. **ERISA Enforcement**

a. ***Section 501 [§ 1131]*** [*]***: Criminal Penalties***—This section provides for fines and/or imprisonment for **willful violators** of ERISA provisions.

b. ***Section 502 [§ 1132]: Civil Enforcement***—This section creates civil causes of action.

i. ***Section 502(a)(1)(B): Recovery of wrongfully denied benefits***—This section entitles pension plan participants and beneficiaries to bring suit to recover benefits they are due, but are wrongfully denied because of

---

[*] Primary section references are to the ERISA act, bracketed references are to the codified section numbering scheme at 29 U.S.C.

violations of § 404, § 510 (*discussed infra*) or other ERISA provisions. Recovered damages in a § 503(a)(1)(B) action go to the plaintiff.

ii. ***Section 502(a)(2): Reporting requirements violation***—This section entitles pension plan participants, beneficiaries, fiduciaries, and the secretary of labor to sue employers for not adhering to the reporting requirements of Title I. As a failure to adhere to reporting requirements is a wrong committed against all plan beneficiaries, any recovery from a § 502(a)(2) suit is awarded to the plan rather than the person bringing suit.

c. ***Section 404 [§ 1103]: Fiduciary Duties***—Pension plans must have a "fiduciary" who will oversee the administration of the plan. While employers are allowed to act as fiduciaries for their own plans—and often do—when they act in this fiduciary capacity, they are required to act **"solely in the interest of participants and beneficiaries."** Thus, employers are prohibited from administering the plan in such a way as to advantage employer interests while working to the detriment of beneficiaries. Beneficiaries may sue for breach of fiduciary duty under § 502.

i. ***Arising conflicts of interest***—Sometimes fiduciaries who are also company or union officials can find themselves in conflict-of-interest situations because of changing circumstances. For instance, if a pension plan holds stock in its own company, and the voting rights of this stock become important in a corporate takeover contest, a special conflict-of-interest situation exists. According to *Donovan v. Bierwith* (2d. Cir. 1982), fiduciaries should **obtain outside, independent advice and temporarily suspend their work as a plan fiduciary**, if necessary, to avoid liability.

ii. ***Deference to fiduciary's interpretation of plan provisions***—*Firestone Tire & Rubber Co. v. Bruch* (U.S. 1989) delineates what standard of review will be used by a court when someone sues for a denial of benefits under a plan. As a default rule, the fiduciary's decision about eligibility for benefits is reviewed *de novo*. However, if the plan provides that the fiduciary is granted discretionary power to interpret the language of the plan, then the fiduciary's interpretation is **entitled to deference unless** the fiduciary's interpretation amounts to an **abuse of power**.

d. ***Section 510 [§ 1140]: Interference with Employee Rights***—ERISA prohibits employers from taking employment actions, such as firing an employee, for the purpose of **interfering with a vested right or preventing the vesting of a right**.

- A **"vested"** right or benefit is one that has been earned by the employee and for which the employee need do nothing further to be entitled to the right. Some pension plans do not vest until the employee has worked for a certain number of years. If the employee quits before the vesting date, no pension benefits will be due the employee.

i. ***Classic violation***—The classic violation of § 510 would be when an employer, in an attempt to avoid the expense of paying retirement benefits, fires an employee a few days before his retirement benefits vest.

If the employer could get away with this, the employer would have gained the advantage of the productivity and loyalty of the employee over the years without having to pay the price for this advantage in the form of disbursing pension benefits.

ii. **_Intent requirement_**—Bringing a successful suit under § 510 is more difficult than it may at first seem. The greatest stumbling block for plaintiffs is the intent requirement—§ 510 only prohibits action undertaken **"for the purpose of"** interfering with the rights of employees.

1) **_Changing health-care coverage_**—In _McGann v. H & H Music Co._ (5th Cir. 1991), an employer capped coverage for AIDS at $5,000 per person in its self-insured health plan _after_ finding out that one of its employees had been diagnosed as HIV positive. The court held that the employer did not intend to injure the employee, but merely was attempting to control the escalating costs of health care, and therefore the employee was not entitled to recover under § 510.

a) N.B.: This controversial holding **may be moot after the passage of the ADA**, which may prohibit the employer's actions as discrimination on the basis of disability.

2) **_Plant closings_**—The circuit courts are split on whether plant closings—selected for the purpose of saving on pensions—are a violation of § 510.

6. **ERISA Preemption**—Section 514 _[§ 1144]_ preempts all state laws that relate to employee benefit plans. ERISA preemption is especially important with regard to welfare benefits; the most noteworthy of which is health care. ERISA's preemption of state regulation of employee health benefits has been widely criticized.

a. **_Text_**—Section 514 states "the provisions ... of this Act shall supersede any and all State laws insofar as they may now or hereafter relate to any employee benefit plan[.]"

b. **_The "Plan" Requirement_**—To be preempted, the regulation must relate to an employee benefit _plan_. Thus, a Maine law that requires a one-time payment of cash benefits to workers laid-off because of a plant closing is not preempted, because the one-time payment does not constitute a "plan." _Fort Halifax Packing Co. v. Coyne_ (U.S. 1987).

c. **_The "Relate To" Requirement_**—The "relate to" language of ERISA has been very broadly interpreted by the Supreme Court.

i. **_Preemption of Benefit Regulation_**—ERISA clearly preempts any state attempt to directly regulate employee benefit plans.

ii. **_Preemption of Laws of General Applicability_**—Even laws of general applicability can be preempted under ERISA. If a person sues an employer because of wrongfully withheld benefits, e.g., on the basis of state contract law or tort law, ERISA will almost always preempt the cause of action.

1) ***The* Pilot Life *Case*:** An employee sued an insurance company under tort and contract theories for improper processing of benefits, where the company terminated and reinstated the employer's disability benefits several times. The state-law claims of action were preempted. *Pilot Life Insurance Co. v. Deadeaux* (U.S. 1987).

2) ***The* Ingersoll-Rand v. McClendon *Case*:** An employee alleged he was fired to avoid the vesting of his pension benefits, and sued for wrongful discharge in violation of public policy, seeking punitive damages and compensatory damages for emotional distress. Despite the fact that the person did not seek recovery of pension benefits, ERISA still preempted the claim of action because of the connection with the benefit plan. *Ingersoll-Rand Co. v. McClendon* (U.S. 1990).

❖ *EXAM TIP:* **Remember to watch out for ERISA preemption issues in exam questions that seem to be primarily about state law.**

iii. ***Insurance/Savings Clause***—Section 514(b)(2)(A) specifically exempts state regulation of insurance, banking, and securities from preemption. This provision is known as the "Insurance/Savings Clause" or simply the "Savings Clause." Because of this clause, states may enact laws that overwhelmingly aim at employer-sponsored health insurance but escape ERISA preemption.

1) ***Broader Than Insurance***—If a law's applicability extends beyond the insurance, banking, or securities industries, then the Insurance/Savings Clause will not shield it from the preemptive effect of ERISA. For instance, common law making actionable bad-faith performance of a contract is law that extends well beyond applicability to the insurance industry. Therefore, such common-law claims of action are preempted when used for wrongs suffered from the administration of a benefit plan. *Pilot Life Insurance Co. v. Deadeaux* (U.S. 1987).

2) **The *Met Life v. Mass* Case**—The Supreme Court held that a state may require all insurance companies to provide mental-health benefits as part of any health-insurance policy sold, even though most health insurance is provided by employers and the law therefore indirectly regulates employee benefit programs. *Metropolitan Life Insurance Co. v. Massachusetts* (U.S. 1985).

iv. ***The Deemer Clause***—The Deemer Clause, § 514(b)(2)(B), clarifies and limits the effect of the Insurance/Savings Clause. **If an employer self-**

insures, the Deemer Clause provides that the employer cannot be considered an "insurer" for purposes of state regulation. *FMC Corp. v Holliday* (U.S. 1990). Thus, a self-insured plan is immune from state laws. Large employers often self-insure to avoid state regulation. This method allows employers to avoid covering certain diseases and to cap coverage for others, despite substantive state insurance regulation that would require the inclusion of those diseases or that limits coverage caps.

D. Health Insurance Portability

1. **Overview**—Recent legislation has provided some substantive regulation of health-care benefits by providing legal rights to continue health insurance as employees change jobs. COBRA focuses on the old employer, allowing employees to continue their health insurance after losing their job. HIPAA focuses on the new employer, limiting the ability of benefit plans to exclude pre-existing conditions or to impose waiting periods.

2. **COBRA**—COBRA, named after a portion of the Consolidated Omnibus Budget Reconciliation Act of 1985, which amended ERISA §§ 601–607 *[29 U.S.C. §§ 1161–1167]*, allows those who receive employment-benefit health insurance to continue coverage under that health insurance after termination of employment or some other "qualifying event." This temporary period of coverage is meant to allow people to secure other health insurance.

   a. *Qualifying Event*—Because many of the recipients of employment-benefit health insurance are not employees, but the spouses or dependents of employees, the definition of qualifying event goes beyond the termination of one's own job. See ERISA § 603 *[§ 1163]*. Qualifying events include:

      1) Death of the employee;

      2) Termination of employment, unless the termination was for the employee's gross misconduct;

      3) Divorce or separation from the spouse-employee;

      4) Becoming too old to qualify as a dependent child.

   b. *COBRA Election*—Those entitled to receive continued coverage must be notified by the employer of their right to do so, and they have 60 days in which to make the election.

   c. *Duration of Coverage*—COBRA coverage must last for up to 18 or 36 months, depending on the circumstances.

   d. *Premiums*—Previous employees may be required to pay premiums for the continued coverage, but the premiums may not be more than 102 percent of the normal premiums, or not more than 150 percent for periods continuing beyond 18 months.

e. ***Coverage of COBRA***—COBRA provisions apply only to employers with 20 or more employees.

3. HIPAA—Enacted in 1996, the Health Insurance Portability and Accountability Act (HIPAA) helps people secure new group health insurance through a variety of means.

    a. ***Restrictions on Group Health Plans***—HIPAA limits the ability of employers and insurers to exclude pre-existing conditions or to impose waiting periods for new applicants.

        i. ***Pre-existing condition exclusions***—HIPAA prohibits group health plans from excluding coverage for pre-existing health conditions for more than 12 months. This exclusion period must be reduced by any periods of creditable coverage.

            1) ***Creditable coverage***—Most kinds of previous health insurance or health benefits can constitute creditable coverage, which reduces the amount of time that a group health plan can exclude pre-existing conditions. If, however, there is a lapse of 63 days between the previous health coverage and the coverage of the new health plan, the previous health insurance does not count as "creditable coverage." COBRA coverage counts as creditable coverage.

            2) ***Example:*** After being without health insurance for a year, Ned takes a job at ChemCo, where he is given membership in a group health plan, but his pre-existing condition for asthma is excluded from coverage for 12 months. After seven months at ChemCo, Ned is laid off. One month later he is hired at Acme Chemicals, which offers employees a group health plan. HIPAA entitles Ned to join the health plan and his asthma can be excluded for no longer than five months (12 months minus seven months of creditable coverage at ChemCo). Note that the time at ChemCo counts as creditable coverage even though Ned's asthma was excluded from coverage at that time.

    b. ***Requirements for Insurers***—Under some circumstances, HIPAA compels insurance companies to sell policies to individuals and employers.

        i. ***Small employers***—Insurers that sell small-group health insurance cannot turn down small employers for coverage and must accept every eligible individual employee into its plan. There are some exceptions for financial hardship of the insurer.

        ii. ***Individuals not covered by group health insurance***—If an insurer sells health coverage to individuals, that insurer cannot deny coverage to eligible persons. To be eligible, a person must have been covered under a group health plan for 18 months. Thus, if someone loses her job and the group health coverage that the job provided, she can secure permanent health insurance even if her new employer does not offer health benefits or even if she does not find a job at all afterwards.

4. **COBRA and HIPAA Together**—Viewed together, COBRA and HIPAA give individuals substantial flexibility to change jobs and respond to unemployment without fear of losing health-insurance coverage. Many commentators view this portability as economically beneficial, because it frees the labor market of the artificial constraints of health-insurance job-lock. COBRA and HIPAA also reflect an understanding of the economics of insurance. By allowing significant time to elapse, persons lose their rights under COBRA and HIPAA. This prevents persons from taking advantage of insurers by not paying premiums when they are healthy but enrolling in insurance plans when they get sick and need coverage.

5. **MHPA**—The Mental Health Parity Act of 1996 (MHPA) was enacted in 1996 and amended ERISA and the Public Health Service Act to provide for parity in the application of certain limits on mental-health benefits with those on medical/surgical benefits.

CHAPTER VIII

THE OCCUPATIONAL SAFETY AND HEALTH ACT

A. Introduction

1. **Overview**—The Occupational Safety and Health Act of 1970 (OSHA) created a federal scheme for regulating workplace safety and health. The Act utilizes both a "general-duty clause," which prohibits dangerous conditions in general, as well as specific standards that regulate in detail what employers in specific industries must do to safeguard workers from various hazards.

2. **Comparison to Workers' Compensation and Tort Law**—OSHA creates an *ex ante* regime for dealing with injuries in the workplace. That is, OSHA works *before* the injury, seeking directly to prevent injuries and disease by forcing employers to create a safer, healthier workplace. Contrast this to workers' compensation laws and tort suits, which are *ex post* regimes—they come into play after the injury or disease has already been suffered. Workers' compensation, tort suits, and OSHA all work to prevent harm to employees. The difference is that OSHA *directly* seeks to prevent harm to workers by setting out safety standards. Workers' comp and tort law can prevent harm *indirectly* where the threat of large verdicts or increased insurance payments persuades employers to make their workplaces safer.

3. **OSHA and OSHA**—Both the Occupational Safety and Health Act, as well as the agency created under it—the Occupational Safety and Health Administration—are referred to by the abbreviation "OSHA."

4. **The Role of the Secretary of Labor**—The OSHA administration is a unit of the Department of Labor. The secretary of labor is usually the named complainant in OSHA cases and is named as the official ultimately responsible for carrying out the rulemaking requirements under the OSHA statute.

5. **No Private Right of Action**—OSHA does not provide for a private right of action. Instead, actions under OSHA must be brought by the secretary of labor and the OSHA administration. While employees can complain to OSHA and the secretary of labor about violations and can request that the administration take action, employees themselves cannot sue the employer.

6. **Coverage**—OSHA applies to all employers in a business affecting interstate commerce. This provision has been interpreted very broadly and reaches almost all employers in the nation, save those specifically exempted. Government agencies and various industries with specific, alternative regulatory schemes are not covered under OSHA, and states may opt out of OSHA if they have created their own approved alternative. Many states have done so.

B. General-Duty Clause

1. Introduction

 a. ***Substantive Law***—Section 5(a) of OSHA is the general-duty clause. While the rest of the OSHA law concerns the administration, enforcement, and promulgation of specific rules, the general-duty clause is substantive law that imposes a direct burden on employers.

 b. ***Text of the General-Duty Clause***—Section 5(a) provides, "Each employer shall furnish to each of his employees employment and a place of employment which are free from recognized hazards that are causing or are likely to cause death or serious physical harm to his employees."

 c. ***Recognized and Preventable***—To take action against an employer under the general-duty clause, **OSHA must show that the hazard was both preventable and recognized.**

2. Recognized—The "recognized" requirement is similar to an intent requirement in torts or criminal law, and it serves to keep the general-duty clause from being applied with strict liability. A hazard is considered "recognized" if it meets ***either*** subjective or objective tests.

 a. ***Objectively Recognized***—A hazard that is recognized by the industry as a whole will be considered recognized for OSHA purposes. Thus, even employers that are ignorant of workplace hazards may be liable for them if such hazards are generally known to professionals in the industry.

 b. ***Subjectively Recognized***—A hazard that is recognized by the employer can establish employer liability even if the industry is generally ignorant of such a danger.

  i. ***Example:*** If a woodshop using a new model of band saw knows that the band can snap off, injuring workers, that employer can be held liable even if no one else in the industry knows of the saw's harmful potential.

 c. ***Accidents Not Required***—Because the statute discusses hazards that are "likely" to cause injury, an accident is not required before an employer will incur the duty to correct the hazard. On the other hand, the occurrence of an accident may serve to make the hazard recognized if the hazard was previously undiscovered.

3. Feasibly Preventable—Although the statute does not use the word "preventable," the law has been interpreted to permit industrial practices that produce hazards that are not feasibly preventable.

 a. ***Feasible***—Remedial measures may be unfeasible because of terrific cost or technological unsoundness. Thus, there may be many dangerous industrial processes that are not affected by the general-duty clause.

 b. ***Effective***—To make the hazard at issue preventable, the proposed safeguard must be demonstrably effective.

4. **Specific Standards are a Defense**—If there is a specific OSHA standard on point for a particular situation, the employer may assume that meeting that specific standard will also satisfy the general-duty clause. If charged with a general-duty violation, an employer may raise this argument as a defense.

   a. *Exception: Standard Known to be Deficient*—If the employer, however, knew that the specific OSHA standard was not stringent enough to prevent a recognized hazard, the defense will fail.

C. Promulgation of Standards

The OSHA law grants the secretary of labor the power to promulgate rules, called "standards," setting specific requirements for workplace safety and health. There are three ways in which rules may have been enacted.

1. **"Interim Standards" Under § 6(a)**—Within a period of two years after its enactment, § 6(a) of OSHA directed the secretary of labor to adopt of rules codifying health or safety standards that existed as a matter of national consensus. This mechanism allowed for the rapid adoption of rules in the beginning of the OSHA's life. These rules have permanent validity, and most OSHA standards on the books now were adopted under § 6(a). Since this interim-rule-enactment period ended in 1973, however, no rules—whether they reflect national consensus or not—can be adopted today through this provision. New rules and any changes to existing § 6(a) rules must be promulgated through § 6(b) or § 6(c).

2. **"New Standards" Under § 6(b)**—New rules may be promulgated according to the method prescribed in § 6(b). The process is onerous, and so few rules have been adopted in this manner.

   a. *Procedural Requirements*—Section 6(b) sets forth a complex process that must be undertaken in order to adopt a new standard. The process requires a period of public review and mandates public hearings with regard to objections.

   b. *Substantive Requirements*—The OSHA act has been interpreted to set substantive limits on the rulemaking authority of the secretary of labor. While lower-court cases have wrestled with many aspects of § 6(b)'s substantive scope, the Supreme Court guidance on the issue has been limited.

      i. *Significant risk / § 3(8) / The Benzene Case*—In order to promulgate new rules under § 6(b), the secretary of labor must meet the burden of proving that there is a *significant risk* **of a material health impairment** for which the proposed standard is reasonably necessary and appropriate. This requirement was set forth in the Benzene Case—*Industrial Union Department, AFL-CIO v. American Petroleum Institute* (U.S. 1980). A plurality opinion identified this requirement from OSHA § 3(8), which provides that a standard must be "reasonably necessary or appropriate to provide safe or healthful employment."

ii. *Feasibility analysis / § 6(b)(5) / The Cotton-Dust Case*—With regard to rules dealing with toxic materials or harmful physical agents, the secretary, under OSHA § 6(b)(5), must promulgate the rule which most assures "to the extent feasible ... that no employee will suffer material impairment of health." In the Cotton-Dust Case—*American Textiles Manufacturers Institute, Inc. v. Donovan* (U.S. 1981)—the Supreme Court rejected the argument that OSHA should show that new standards are justified by a cost-benefit analysis. Instead, the proposed standard must be technologically and economically feasible.

- N.B.: The feasibility analysis of the Cotton-Dust Case applies only to "health" regulation, and not to "safety" regulation. So while it applies to standards for exposures to toxic substances, for example, it does not apply to standards about scaffolding or machinery guards. Lower courts have sometimes required even stricter analysis for safety standards.

  1) *Technologically feasible*—The method of eliminating the hazard must be technologically possible; that is, a merely hypothetical solution does not meet the feasibility requirement.

  2) *Economically feasible*—To be economically feasible, a solution must not be so expensive that it would force most of the industry into bankruptcy. On the other hand, the elimination of a hazard might still be feasible even if it is prohibitively expensive to some firms. Thus, some firms may be forced out of operation because of a solution that is judged to be feasible.

3. **"Emergency Temporary Standards" Under § 6(c)**—Section 6(c) allows the secretary to adopt emergency temporary standards.

   a. *Procedural Requirement*—A new rule promulgated under 6(c) is effective immediately upon its publication in the Federal Register. The rule is effective, however, for only six months, after which the rule must be replaced by a § 6(b) permanent rule; otherwise it will lapse.

   b. *Substantive Requirements*—Section 6(c) rules must meet a **two-prong substantive test**. The secretary may only promulgate such a rule when he or she finds that the rule **is necessary to protect workers** from a **"grave danger"** created by new hazards or toxic or harmful substances. The grave-danger prong has been interpreted not to require a finding of certainty of impending harm, but to require "more than some possibility."

D. Enforcement

1. **Inspections**—Inspections of work sites by OSHA officials may be triggered by accidents at that work site, by employee complaints, or as part of a program of random inspections. While employers may require a warrant for the entry of OSHA

officials, there is no requirement for OSHA officials to show probable cause to obtain a warrant.

2. **Remedies**—Upon the recommendation of an inspector, an OSHA official may calculate fines, prescribe abatement for the hazardous condition, and issue a citation.

3. **OSHRC**—The employer may contest the fine and abatement with a timely filing to the Occupational Safety and Health Review Commission (OSHRC), a body outside the Department of Labor. After a hearing of the employer and OSHA, an administrative law judge renders judgment.

4. **Appeals**—Either the employer or OSHA may appeal an adverse ruling to the U.S. Court of Appeals for the circuit in which the violation was alleged to have occurred.

5. **Private Parties**—While OSHA rules are promulgated and enforced by the secretary of labor through the OSHA administration, the act does have implications for individual employees.

   a. *No Private Right of Action*—Remember that OSHA does not create a private right of action, and only the secretary of labor, through the OSHA administration, may take legal action under OSHA. No other parties can sue or take legal action against employers under OSHA.

   b. *Employee Complaints*—Employees can complain to OSHA, either individually or through their union, and request that OSHA make inspections and/or initiate legal action.

   c. *Protection from Retaliation Against Employees*—Section 11(c) of the OSHA statute prohibits employers from firing or otherwise retaliating against employees for actions taken in regard to workplace safety and health issues, including

      1) Complaining to OSHA;

      2) Refusing to perform work that the employee reasonably believes, in good faith, to present the danger of death or serious injury;

      3) Taking other actions with regard to health and safety on the job.

   Like all other provisions of OSHA, § 11(c) does not create a private right of action. Therefore, employees who are the victims of alleged retaliation can request OSHA to take action on their behalf, but cannot sue under OSHA.

E. The Employee-Misconduct Defense

1. **Generally**—Where the dangerous condition giving rise to the violation was created by employees and was not reasonably preventable by the employer, the employer may assert the employee-misconduct defense.

2. **Four-Part Test**—To assert the employee-misconduct defense, the employer must meet a four-part test. *Jensen Construction Co.* (OSHRC 1979).

a. Since the violation, the employer has established rules to prevent further violations;

b. These rules have been adequately communicated to workers;

c. The employer has attempted to discover unknown violations;

d. The employer has corrected violations when they have been discovered.

3. **Additional Considerations**—While the *Jensen Construction* four-part test focuses more on the employer's overall safety program, courts also scrutinize the violation itself. Thus, courts also look to whether the violation at issue was isolated, caused by an employee, unknown to the employer, and contrary to the employer's instructions and uniformly enforced workplace rules.

CHAPTER IX

WORKERS' COMPENSATION

A. Introduction

1. **History**—During the industrial revolution, various evolutions of tort law made it increasingly difficult for employees to recover from their employers for injuries suffered in the workplace. In addition to establishing the negligence of the employer, a worker had to show that he had not *assumed the risk* of the employment or *contributed to the negligence* that caused the injury-producing accident.

2. **The Workers' Compensation Solution**—States enacted workers' compensation regimes that shield employers from large awards of punitive and compensatory damages in tort suits and at the same time make it much easier for workers to recover some compensation.

3. **Negligence Not Required**—Employees may recover workers' compensation benefits regardless of whether the employer was negligent.

4. **Causation Standard Different**—Rather than traditional tort concepts of causation, workers' compensation is awarded based on the concept of "in the course of and arising out of employment."

5. **Benefits**—Workers' compensation benefits include payment of medical bills for the injury and disability benefits, which are usually calculated as a fraction of lost wages.

6. **Funding**—Employers can either pay premiums into a workers' compensation insurance fund or they can choose to self-insure. If employers opt for insurance coverage, the premiums are experience-based, so that employers with higher-accident rates will pay more in premiums.

7. **The Workers' Compensation Trade-off**—Workers' compensation schemes involve a trade-off for both workers and employers.

   a. *For workers*, workers' compensation allows recovery regardless of employer negligence. This means that workers need not go through the difficult and expensive process of trying to prove that the employer was at fault for the injury. Additionally, workers can claim benefits for non-negligent injuries that the tort system would never provide. The disadvantage for workers is that their recovery is limited, often to two-thirds of lost wages. Also, permanent disabilities, such as the loss of a limb, are subject to maximum benefit caps, meaning that even as the worker continues to suffer from the injury, workers' compensation benefits may run out.

   b. *For employers*, workers' compensation limits their liability, shielding them from large recoveries in lawsuits. Although employers avoid the risk of large losses sustained in legal actions, they must pay a regular premium to the state's workers-compensation fund. The premiums are experienced-based, so that dangerous firms must pay more. Nonetheless, a disadvantage for safe firms is that even where employees suffer zero injuries, the company will still be required to pay minimum premiums to the workers' compensation fund, unless they can self-insure.

> *FOR BETTER UNDERSTANDING:* Because of the trade-off involved in workers' compensation, the **employers and employees may find themselves on different sides of the question of whether workers' compensation should be granted**. An employer trying to avoid paying workers' compensation benefits may argue that an accident is not covered by workers' compensation. An employee, however, may also argue that an injury is not covered by workers' compensation if that employee is attempting to open up the possibility suing the employer in tort.

B. Requirements for Obtaining Benefits

A claim for workers' compensation is subject to a four-prong test. For an employee to obtain workers' compensation benefits, there must be a:

i.   Personal injury;

ii.   Resulting from an accident;

iii.   That occurs during the course of employment;

iv.   And arises out of employment.

The course-of-employment requirement deals with the time, place, and circumstances of the activity and associated injury. The arising-out-of-employment requirement is concerned with the causation question: Can the employment be said to be the cause of the accident?

Each of these requirements is explored in detail below.

1. **Personal Injury**—While most injuries are clearly compensable, the "personal injury" requirement becomes a point of contention when the injury involved includes a component of mental illness.

    a. *Physical-Physical*—Where both the cause and the effect are physical, the harm will be considered a personal injury.

        i.   *Example:* Where a blackjack dealer loses a finger because a security camera fell from the ceiling, the physical-physical injury is compensable.

    b. *Physical-Mental*—Where the cause is physical and the effect is physical and mental, the vast majority of states will consider the condition to be an "injury" for purposes of determining compensability.

        i.   *Example:* If a security camera falls on the blackjack dealer causing her to lose her arm and she therefore suffers a nervous breakdown, the mental consequence is considered an injury in most states.

c. *Mental-Physical*—If the cause is mental, and the effect is physical, most courts will consider the physical injury to be a compensable personal injury.

    i.   *Example:* If the stress of being held at gunpoint during a casino robbery causes a blackjack dealer to inflict self-injury which mangles the fingers she uses to deal cards, most jurisdictions would allow compensation.

d. *Mental-Mental*—Cases in which both the cause and the effect are mental, and there is no accompanying physical cause or effect, the injury requirement is not usually met. Jurisdictions vary in their treatment of mental-mental cases.

2. **Resulting from an Accident**—"Accident" may be defined in some states as a sudden, unexpected occurrence that happens in a particular place at a particular time. Using such a definition, some states have interpreted the accident requirement to exclude conditions that develop over a long period of time—such as disease arising from long-term exposure to hazardous materials, including asbestos-linked cancer.

3. **Course of Employment**—An injury must arise during the course of employment to be covered by workers' compensation. In general, activities that happen when one is working are covered; those that occur when one is not working are not covered. Case law has focused on situations that do not clearly fall into either category.

  a. *Recreational Activities*—Employer-sponsored recreational activities, such as company softball games, may or may not be covered by workers' compensation.

    i.   *The "reasonable expectancy" test*—If the employee was expected to be involved in the recreational activity, then the activity is covered by workers' compensation.

    ii.   *Subjective/objective components must be met*—For the activity to be covered, it must be the case that reasonable employees would believe that they were expected to participate in the activity (objective) and that the employee in this particular case actually thought that participation was expected (subjective).

    iii.   *Facts relevant to a finding of "reasonable expectancy" include:*

      1)   Encouragement or pressure from the employer;

      2)   Involvement by the employer in the activity;

      3)   Benefit to the employer (e.g., "team-building").

    iv.   *Example:* A summer associate at a law firm is hurt while she is playing softball for the firm's team. The firm organized the team and encouraged participation in order to build camaraderie. Furthermore, without the participation of three females, the team would be forced to forfeit the game. Because of the encouragement, involvement, and benefit to the employer, the activity is covered by workers' compensation. *Ezzy v. Workers' Compensation Appeals Board* (Cal. App. 1983).

  b. *Horseplay*—Rubberband fights, roughhousing, and other horseplay activities in the workplace are usually covered by workers' compensation.

i.   ***The "aggressor defense"***—While bystanders injured by horseplay are almost always covered, the employer may show that the person injured in the horseplay was a perpetrator of the conduct. A perpetrator can be considered to have temporarily "abandoned employment," making the conduct ineligible for workers' compensation coverage because the abandonment means the injury did not arise "during the course of employment" and benefits are therefore unavailable. Courts may, however, extend benefits to perpetrators of the horseplay based on the connection of the horseplay to the work environment.

    1)   ***Bystanders***—Some courts decline to recognize a difference between participants and bystanders, finding that if the horseplay is a natural byproduct of a stressful work environment, all workers are covered.

c. ***Commuting and Travel***

i.   ***The coming-and-going rule***—Injuries sustained while commuting are generally not covered by workers' compensation, since workers' compensation regimes are not intended to protect employees from the general perils of life outside the workplace. The "coming-and-going" rule holds that injuries sustained while coming to and going away from work do not arise during the course of employment. Coverage usually begins when the worker enters the employer's property.

ii. ***Exceptions***—This rule is inapplicable (or excepted) in several circumstances:

    1)   ***Necessary passages and noncontiguous spaces***—If employees must traverse a certain stretch of land in order to get to work, the employee may be awarded compensation for accidents occurring on that land. An exceptional danger posed by traversing that space will further increase the likelihood of coverage.

        a)   ***Example:*** If an employee worked as a fish packer at the end of a public pier, and the employee had to come to work when traversing the pier was made dangerous by storm conditions and high waves, then injuries sustained on the pier would be covered.

    2)   ***Special hazards near employer property***—Although jurisdictions vary, courts will sometimes award compensation for injuries caused because employees are exposed to hazardous conditions on public spaces near the employer's property.

    3)   ***Returning to work***—When an employee must make a special trip from home during off-duty hours, such as coming back to the workplace to lock a door or turn off a machine, injuries sustained in transit are usually covered.

4)   ***Travel on employer-owned conveyances***—If the employer provides buses or other vehicles for commuting employees, injuries are usually covered.

5)   ***Vehicle required at work***—If the employee drives a vehicle to work because the vehicle is required during working hours to carry out certain work-related tasks, the commute is usually covered.

iii.   ***Travel for Work***—If the employee travels for work, such as on sales trips or to conferences, compensation is always available for injuries sustained during the performance of work-related tasks. Increasingly often, courts are awarding compensation for injuries sustained while dressing, eating, and bathing during the time in which the worker stays in hotel accommodations, since these tasks are considered essential to work-related travel.

1)   Activities undertaken on a business trip, which are of an exclusively personal nature and not necessary to work performed on the business trip, are generally not covered by the workers' compensation regime.

4. **Arising Out of Employment**—This requirement of workers' compensation coverage deals with the issue of causation. Whether or not a certain injury must be compensated depends on the category of risk into which the injury falls.

a.   ***Types of Risk***—There are three general categories of risk. The vast majority of cases fall into the categories of occupational risk or personal risk, and are therefore easily resolved without further analysis.

    i.   Occupational risks—*always compensable.*

    ii.   Personal risks—*never compensable.*

    iii.   Neutral risks—*sometimes compensable.*

       1)   Only injuries associated with a "neutral risk" require further analysis (discussed *infra* at IX.C.2.d) to determine whether or not they are compensable.

b.   ***Occupational Risks***—Also called "employment risks," occupational risks are those that are directly related to the job at hand. The potential of a factory machine to break and injure a nearby worker is clearly an occupational risk.

c.   ***Personal Risks***—Succumbing to a heart attack caused by arteriosclerosis while at work would not be covered, because the risk of suffering such a heart attack, caused by poor nutrition, lack of exercise, and genetic propensity, has nothing to do with work.

d.   ***Neutral Risks***—So-called "neutral risks" are those that are not clearly occupational or personal. Examples include acts of nature and assaults by strangers. Various jurisdictions use different doctrines in evaluating the facts of particular case and deciding whether or not to award compensation.

- *These doctrines are presented from the least liberal in providing for compensation to the most liberal. This order also mirrors the general historical trend of increasing willingness of courts to grant compensation.*

i. ***Proximate-cause doctrine***—This doctrine is borrowed from tort law. To satisfy the proximate-cause test, the worker must prove that there is an unbroken chain of causation, without intervening causes, which links an employer action to a foreseeable harm for the worker. Given that workers' compensation is intended to have broader coverage than tort law, this doctrine is seemingly inappropriate and is scarce in contemporary cases.

ii. ***Peculiar-risk doctrine***—To satisfy this test, the risk must be "peculiar" to the workplace and not present for members of the general public. Thus, steam burns from boilers would be compensable, but a delivery person's injuries sustained in an automobile accident would not be compensable, since the public-at-large is exposed to the hazards of auto accidents. Modern courts have largely abandoned this doctrine.

iii. ***Increased-risk doctrine***—Less severe than the peculiar-risk doctrine, the increased-risk doctrine demands only that the risk must be greater than that borne by members of the general public. Under this doctrine, a person charged with sitting in a crow's nest in South Florida would suffer an increased chance of being hit by lightning than the average member of the public, and her lightning-burn injury would be compensated. Likewise, a delivery person who spent eight-hours a day on roads with high-accident rates would suffer an increased risk of auto accidents compared to most people, and therefore would be compensated under an increased-risk test.

    1) ***Specific statutory inclusion of accidents on public thoroughfares***—Note that workers not employed primarily as drivers, but only required to drive occasionally as a part of their jobs, would have a difficult time showing increased risk. Thus in many increased-risk states, statutes specify that injuries sustained while traveling in the course of employment will be covered.

iv. ***Actual-risk doctrine***—As long as the risk is one that actually accompanies employment, the resultant injury will be compensated regardless of whether workers have a higher chance of being injured in this particular way than the general public does. For instance, tripping over an electrical cord that the worker installed in order to operate a computer would be an actual risk of employment, even though the risk might be the same or less than that suffered by the general public. This doctrine has been adopted by a large number of states.

v. ***Positional-risk doctrine***—Any injury which would not have been sustained but for the fact that the employee was in a certain place at a certain time because of his employment is covered under the positional-risk doctrine. A meteor-impact at the office would qualify, for instance, since the worker would not have been at the office but for the fact that he was employed there. This is the applicable doctrine in a growing minority of jurisdictions.

    1)   Note that while the positional-risk doctrine is very permissive, it is not the same as a repudiation of the arising-out-of-employment requirement. Many personal risks—such as a heart attack caused by arteriosclerosis—would strike an employee whether at work or elsewhere, and therefore are uncompensable under the positional-risk doctrine.

5. Arising-Out-of-Employment and Course-of-Employment considered together—Some courts hold that a strong case for arising-out-of-employment will offset a weak showing for the course-of-employment requirement.

    a. *Example:* When very long hours without rest and/or where exposure to drowsiness-inducing chemicals causes the worker to fall asleep while driving home, the injury may be compensable despite the fact that the accident happened during the commute and therefore would normally fall under the coming-and-going rule.

C. Typology of Benefits

1. Introduction—There are two basic types of benefits: the provision of medical and rehabilitation care, and the payment of cash to compensate for lost-earnings capacity because of disability or death. The touchstone for workers' compensation benefits is *earning capacity*. Benefits are not calculated to compensate the worker for the harm the injury will have on her greater well being, but rather the effect on her ability to work and earn wages.

2. Medical and Rehabilitation Care Benefits—Workers' compensation will typically pay for the entire amount of medical care and rehabilitation required for the worker's recovery. However, if the worker reaches a plateau of recovery, where she has not been fully restored to her pre-accident health, but appears not to be capable of getting better, many regimes will cease to provide medical and rehabilitation benefits, allowing the worker to receive disability benefits if she is eligible.

3. Cash Payments for Disability and Death—To compensate a worker—at least partially—for lost wages, the worker is given cash payments. Benefits may be disbursed under five statuses:

    a. *Temporary Partial Disability*—Workers who temporarily suffer reduced earnings may be paid a fraction of their lost wages.

    b. *Temporary Total Disability*—Where a worker cannot work at all for a limited time, cash payments equal to some percentage of wages will be paid to the worker.

c. *Permanent Partial Disability*—A worker who can work, but has a permanent condition that will reduce earnings capacity, may receive permanent partial disability payments. These may come in two varieties:

    i. *Scheduled*—States have lists of set rates of disability payments for the loss of various limbs and for other impairments and diseases. Using a scheduled-benefit scheme, disabled workers receive a set amount of money for their lost limb or injury, without regard to their actual reduction in earnings capacity.

    ii. *Unscheduled*—Some injuries are not compensated according to a schedule or chart, but are calculated according to the circumstances of the individual case.

d. *Permanent Total Disability*—The status of permanent total disability applies to workers who will never be able to work again, even in a partial capacity. Permanent total disability payments are usually based on lost earnings capacity.

e. *Death*—When a worker is killed through a work-related accident, workers' compensation may provide death benefits to the dependents of the worker.

D. Exclusivity/Preclusion

1. **General Rule**—Workers' compensation is intended to be the **exclusive means of recovery for a worker against the employer**, thus workers' compensation precludes the possibility of tort suits against employers. There, are however, exceptions to this rule.

2. **Exceptions**

    a. *Intentional Wrongs*—If the employer intentionally injured the employee, then a tort suit may go forward.

        i. *Genuine intentional wrongs*—If the injury is the result of a genuine intentional wrong, there is no tort immunity.

            1) In some courts, if the employer created a condition in which the employer knew or should have known that there was a **substantial certainty** that injury would result, then the wrong is considered intentional.

        ii. *Reckless or wanton acts*—In some courts, reckless or wanton behavior by an employer is not covered by workers' compensation and thus a tort suit may go forward. In other jurisdictions, reckless or wanton acts are covered by the workers' compensation scheme and are shielded from tort liability.

        iii. *Fraudulent concealment*—Where company doctors discover an employee's illness, but do not inform the employee, a theory of fraudulent concealment may allow a suit for worsening of the condition caused by a delay in proper medical treatment. The underlying condition, however, would still be barred by the exclusivity provision, unless it fell under another exception.

b. ***Dual Capacity***—In some states an employee may sue her employer if she is injured when the employer acts in a non-employer capacity. For instance, in some jurisdictions, a person employed by a physician may sue the physician for medical malpractice when the injuries result from the physician/patient relationship rather than the employer/employee relationship.

c. ***Third-Party Defendants***—Employees are sometimes free to sue parties other than the employer, such as contractors, suppliers, and other employees, although jurisdictions vary. Occasionally, these third parties can sue the employer for contribution toward the judgment, meaning that employers may end up with tort liability despite workers-compensation/tort immunity.

    i. ***Third-party plaintiffs***, such as spouses or children of workers, are ordinarily barred from suing the employer in tort, just as the worker is.

d. ***Federal Causes of Action***—If an employee is specifically authorized to sue under a federal statute, such as Title VII, the suit may go forward. State workers' compensation schemes cannot bar suits under federal law.

3. **Preclusion Without Recovery**—In some jurisdictions it is possible for a tort suit to be precluded even when workers' compensation is not awarded. This is because the tort-preclusion aspect works separately from the scheme that determines whether compensation will be awarded. Thus, an injury arising out of and in the course of employment will trigger the preclusive aspect of a workers-compensation statute. If the injury is unaccompanied by an industrial liability, it will not be compensable by disability benefits.

    i. ***Example:*** If a factory worker suffers an accident that gives her disfiguring burns, some workers' compensation regimes would not award benefits to the worker since the disfigurement does not affect her ability to work. Additionally, the worker could not receive disability benefits or tort-like compensation for pain and suffering or emotional distress absent intentional wrongdoing on the part of the employer. The worker would, however, ordinarily be able to receive medical benefits from workers' compensation to cover the cost of treatment for the condition.

CHAPTER X

UNEMPLOYMENT INSURANCE

A. Introduction

1. **Overview**—Unemployment insurance allows people who lose their job through no fault of their own to receive temporary pay while they are looking for a new job. Unlike other law related to employment, unemployment insurance is not primarily concerned with laying blame or punishing certain conduct. Whether an employer had no reason to fire an employee, or a good reason to fire an employee, unemployment insurance is generally available regardless. The primary mission of unemployment insurance is indeed to be *insurance*, that is, to prepare people against the unexpected calamity of unemployment by keeping them afloat financially until they can secure other work. Despite its insurance-oriented mission, it is nonetheless true that the system has important collateral effects of incentivizing certain conduct. This occurs through the effects of adjustable insurance premiums and varying methods of determining eligibility for employees.

2. **History**—The current unemployment-insurance system owes its existence to both federal and state government. The Social Security Act of 1935 imposed a federal unemployment tax on employers, but provided for an offsetting tax credit for employers who paid into a qualifying state unemployment compensation program. This spurred the creation of unemployment compensation systems in all 50 states and the District of Columbia, saving employers money since they could receive the entire federal tax credit while paying less than the federal rate into state unemployment-insurance systems. The current federal scheme is governed by the Federal Unemployment Tax Act (FUTA).

3. **Federal and State Involvement**—FUTA requires minimum standards for state systems, which must be met for employers in those states to receive the federal tax credit. Included are standards for what employers and employees are to be covered by the unemployment-insurance system.

4. **Covered Employers and Employees**

   a. *Employer Coverage*—The general standard is that any employer that pays more than $1,500 in wages in any quarter, or that employed at least one worker on at least one day each of 20 weeks, must pay into the unemployment-insurance system. Different standards apply to agricultural, domestic, and non-profit employers.

   b. *Employee Coverage*—Only workers who are "employees" are covered. (See Chapter I for a discussion of the meaning of "employees.")

B. Assessments Against Employers

1. **Experience Rating**—In order to discourage layoffs and to allocate the costs of the system to those who are most responsible for unemployment, taxation assessments against employers are adjusted to reflect the firm's experience in discharging workers. Two systems are widely used by the states.

   a. *Reserve Ratio*—Under a reserve-ratio system, each employer has an ongoing account with the state unemployment insurance agency, and benefits paid to former employees are charged against the account. Assessments are lowered if the account retains a sufficient balance, or raised if the account balance dips too low.

   b. *Benefit Ratio*—Each employer is assessed contributions based on an average of the last three years of benefits received by former employees.

2. **Limits on Experience Rating**—Although experience rating can connect the cost-burden of the unemployment insurance with employer responsibility for creating unemployment, several common features of a state's unemployment-insurance system can serve to undermine or enhance this tying effect.

   a. *Noncharged Benefits*—Sometimes benefits will not be charged against an employer, when, for instance, an employee is being retrained or has voluntarily quit for family reasons that the state determines not to be the fault of the employer.

   b. *Maximum Tax Rate*—The law may provide for a maximum tax rate. Therefore, some employers who have a history of laying off many employees will reach this maximum rate and thereafter will not pay more in tax even as they lay off increasing numbers of employees.

   c. *Charges Against Multiple Employers*—In some jurisdictions, an unemployed person's benefits may be charged against employers prior to the last employer. Thus, even if an employee voluntarily left the second-to-the-last employer, that employer may be charged for part of the benefits even though it was not the firm that fired the employee.

3. **Economic Theory of Experience Rating and Incentives to Employers**—Employers are normally incentivized to hire workers when their need for labor is great and then fire workers when demand lessens. Experience-rated unemployment insurance changes this economic equation, forcing employers to bear some of the societal costs of unemployment. This system is, however, imperfect. Some stable industries, such as finance and real estate, end up paying more into the system than the amount taken out in benefits by their employees. Seasonal industries, on the other hand, such as construction, generally pay less into the system than is taken out in benefits by their former employees. This means that other industries may end up subsidizing the labor costs of seasonal industries.

C. Eligibility for Employees

The unemployment-insurance system is not intended to work as a welfare system that distributes benefits according to need. Thus, the features of the regime differentiate it from a welfare system.

1. **Previous Work Requirement**—To be eligible for benefits, an employee must have worked for a certain amount of time prior to applying. Usually this period is two or more quarters. This means, for example, that persons having just graduated from college with no work history are ineligible. Benefits are calculated according to the employee's lost salary and are usually about 50 percent of past wages.

2. **Qualifying Discharge**—Employees are generally only eligible for unemployment-insurance benefits if their leaving work was involuntary and not because of misconduct. It is not necessary, however, for the employee to have been laid off; i.e., the employee may have been fired for cause and still be eligible for benefits. Employees might resign and still be eligible for benefits if their resignation was forced or if outside circumstances required their resignation.

   a. *Voluntary Discharge*—The law varies greatly from state to state regarding in which situation employees may voluntarily quit and still be eligible for unemployment benefits. There are, however, two basic models.

      i. *Good cause*—Some jurisdictions will allow an employee to quit and collect benefits if the employee had "good cause" for quitting. For instance, leaving a job to care for a chronically ill child or to follow a spouse to a new job in a new location may be considered "good cause." When a quit is said to be for "good cause," it is considered "involuntary" under the circumstances, making the employee eligible for benefits.

      ii. *Good cause attributable to the employer*—Some states require that the reason for the quit be attributable to the employer in order for the employee to be eligible for benefits. For instance, quitting to take care of a sick child would disqualify the employee from receiving benefits, but quitting because of sexual harassment at work might be excused. States following this doctrine generally use an objective standard for determining eligibility—the condition at work must be of such a nature that it would cause **the reasonable person** to resign.

   b. *Employee Misconduct*—Even when an employee is involuntarily discharged, the employee will not be able to collect benefits if the firing is because of the employee's misconduct. States' laws vary widely on what will be considered misconduct.

      • *Examples:* A worker being fired for saying his employer was "brain dead" and an employee who drove a 10"4' truck into a 10"2' underpass were deemed eligible, but a worker who used an anti-Semitic insult and an employee who had eight accidents in six months were both deemed ineligible on account of willful misconduct.

i. ***Constitutional issues***—An employee who is fired for refusing to work certain days because of religious observances may not be denied benefits under the First Amendment's Free Exercise Clause, even though the employer may have acted legally in firing the employee.

ii. ***Addiction and willful misconduct***—While drinking or drug use may be willful misconduct, if the behavior is deemed to be caused by an addiction disorder, it may be construed as being non-volitional and therefore not willful misconduct.

c. ***Searching for Employment***—As a continuing condition of receiving benefits, the unemployed person **must search for and apply for comparable work**. A physician must look for other work as a physician, for instance, but will not be required to apply for a job taking tickets at a movie theater.

i. ***Personal appearance***—Persons may be denied benefits if they do not keep an adequate personal appearance that would be expected of comparable employers.

ii. ***Holding out for rehire***—Employees may (or may not) be excused from searching for another job if their lay off is temporary and their rehire is imminent.

d. ***Refusing Suitable Employment***—Generally, employees will lose eligibility for benefits for refusing an offer of suitable employment. At the point they refuse such an offer, their unemployment is considered to be purely voluntary.

i. ***Setting a higher standard for the next job***—Some courts will allow persons to refuse jobs comparable to their previous job because of changing needs, such as requiring different hours so that they may take care of children.

D. Administration and Review

1. **Filing Procedure**—Administration of unemployment benefits is handled through public unemployment offices where unemployed workers may file for benefits by providing information about their recent job loss and their previous employment history. The employer also files information about the termination.

2. **Administrative Review**—Benefit determination can be challenged either by applicants or by employers whose accounts are being charged. An administrative official or commission can be called upon to review or referee challenges, and a further appeal is available to a final administrative appeals body.

3. **Judicial Review**—After a final administrative determination, aggrieved parties may file suit in state court for judicial review. Depending on the jurisdiction, courts may undertake a *de novo* review of the case or may accord considerable deference to the factual findings and/or legal determinations of the administrative body.

REVIEW QUIZ

I. WHO IS AN EMPLOYEE?

1. Eugene works for TEJ Company as a surplus salesperson. TEJ Co. dumps many surplus items from its warehouses into a corner of its lot, and Eugene sells as many of the items as he can. Eugene decides what the hours will be, deals with buyers who come around, and makes up the prices to be charged. He gets to keep 20 percent of all sales revenue. Is Eugene an employee of TEJ Co.?

2. Same as the previous facts, but TEJ Co. requires the surplus lot to be open from 10 to 4 every day, and compensates Eugene with a $6-an-hour wage. Is Eugene an employee?

3. Kate works days during the summer at Montreaux Casuals in the mall. She is paid a 10-percent commission on all clothing that she sells, unless that compensation falls below minimum wage, in which case she is given the minimum wage for all hours worked. Is Kate an employee?

4. In the autumn, Kate goes back to school and starts working for TeleLink Long Distance. She sets up a table on her college campus and gives away TeleLink highlighters and t-shirts to people who sign up. She gets a $25 commission for each person she signs up for the service. Kate also often buys granola bars out of her own pocket to give away to passers-by to attract attention to her table. Kate's contract says that TeleLink can tell her exactly what to give out and exactly where and when to set up her table, but in practice, TeleLink has let her make all the decisions. Is Kate an employee?

5. Ed works as a technical writer at Ahab Biotech, Inc., a company famous for giving all employees lucrative stock options. Ed signed a contract that says he is an independent contractor and not an employee, and thus, he does not receive any stock options. After talking to a friend who took an employment law course, Ed becomes convinced, that because of the constant supervision and employment-like working conditions at Ahab, he is really an employee. Can Ed be awarded the value of stock options?

II. DISCHARGE

1. Ted is an at-will employee of T&E Company. Can Ted leave without giving two weeks notice—that is, without incurring damages?

2. Bob is an employee of Speedway General Store, and he has a contract with the store that provides he will be fired only for just cause. The store is located in Arkassippi, an at-will state. Bob is fired for "looking funny" at the boss. In a lawsuit over the discharge, who will prevail?

3. Goldie works at the Grand Leader Department Store under a contract allowing discharge only for just cause. Her boss and several other employees conspire to make

her quit, and after enduring three weeks of constant harassment from these workers, Goldie finally quits. Can she sue for wrongful discharge?

4. Same as the previous, but there is no evidence that her boss and the other employees intended to make her quit. Can she still sue for wrongful discharge?

5. Dylan, a morning disc jockey, has a three-year contract with KMSD. After a year, a different radio station fires the famous Crazy Bob, and KMSD's management wants to fire Dylan to make room for Crazy Bob at KMSD. Are they free to do so?

6. Sarah has a two-year contract to work as a small-business loan officer for MegaBank. The loan market slumps because small entrepreneurs are using credit cards rather than traditional loans. MegaBank is therefore terminating its small-business loan department. Can MegaBank fire Sarah before two years are up?

7. Jared has a contract with the Kanorado Kayfubs, a double-A baseball team. The contract states only that he will be paid $3100 a month. In July, after two days on the job, the Kayfubs fire Jared and give him $200 as his pay. Can Jared sue for breach of contract?

8. Rico has a $2.5-million-a-year/three-year contract to host enormously popular television game-show "Who Wants to be Embarrassed in Front of Millions of People?" Rico quits after a year, and the production company hires Joe at $3 million a year to replace him. What can the production company recover, if anything, from Rico?

9. Danielle has a contract to perform figure skating for one-night only at the Midwestern Ice Festival. The festival promotes Danielle's performance and sells out the CornDome. A week before the event, Danielle announces she will not perform, even though she is fully capable of doing so. Can the festival get an injunction to make her perform?

10. Jamie is fired from Yen Ching restaurant in breach of his contract. He looks for work for a week, but then stops, counting on a lawsuit against Yen Ching to provide income. Can Jaime recover the full salary he would have been collecting at Yen Ching?

11. Jutta, who makes $30,000 a year as a third grade teacher at Konigswald, a private elementary school, is fired after six months, despite her two-year contract. Jutta looks for other elementary-school teaching positions, but she cannot find any within commuting distance of her home. Desperate for cash, she takes a job at a yogurt store in the mall six months after losing her teaching job. At the yogurt store, Jutta earns $12,000 in a year. How much may Jutta recover in a lawsuit against Konigswald School?

12. HarborLink Ferries distributes an employment manual to its workforce, which specifies a just-cause standard for discharge. The manual says on the front page in large bold letters: "Nothing herein is a promise or guarantee. This manual contains guidelines only for managerial purposes and does not form any sort of contract with employees." Is the manual a valid contract?

13. Alisa, a pilot for TransOceanic Air, is offered a higher salary by Intercontinental Airways. The chief of flight operations at Intercontinental tells Alisa that they never let go of pilots because of hard economic times. Concerned about the strength of the economy and her job security at TransOceanic, Alisa goes to work for Intercontinental.

When a recession drives down fares, Alisa is fired. Can she successfully sue for breach of contract?

14. In the state of Nevachusetts, Dean is asked to work all day on election day and to stay on employee premises during his half-hour meal breaks. Dean leaves work for a few minutes during lunch to vote and is subsequently fired. Nevachusetts has no specific law requiring employers to give time off for voting. Does Dean have a claim?

15. Gretchen, believing that Ultra Yum Donuts, her employer, is in substantial violation of the health code, calls county public health authorities about her concerns. Gretchen is fired. Does she have a claim?

16. Speedy Delivery Co. provides delivery services exclusively in downtown Pittsburgh. Two weeks after taking over as the CEO of Speedy, Tim fires half of Speedy's 80-person workforce to cut costs. Do the fired workers have a claim?

17. Kit, an IRS agent with a very strong record of securing payment of back taxes, is fired shortly after anti-tax crusader Steve Flubs takes office as president. Flubs says Kit's very success on the job shows her incompatibility with the Flubs' administration philosophy. Is the discharge proper?

18. Laura is a tenured agriculture professor at Nebrasota State University. The chancellor, dean, and the faculty committee meet and decide that because of Laura's substantial lack of scholarship and extremely high levels of dissatisfaction among students, Laura must be fired. Laura is informed of the decision and told to pack up her things and leave. Does Laura have a claim against the public university?

III. EMPLOYEE DUTIES AND OBLIGATIONS

1. Jim, a ticket seller for Millenium Cinemas, has told several customers who asked for tickets to *The Screaming Halloween Witch Project IV* that the movie really stinks and they'd be better off renting a video for the night. Can the movie theater recover?

2. Troy, the webmaster at Chewinggum.com, tells several customers that he is thinking about starting his own competing service called Gumworld.net. Does Chewinggum.com have a claim against Troy?

3. Florence, the manager of the Livingston Funeral Home, is approached by Teksacani Funeral Home, which is looking to be bought out. Florence quits Livingston and buys Teksacani herself. Does Livingston have a claim?

4. Claire, a chef for Tchotschky's Restaurants, signed a non-compete agreement to not work for any other employer in the food or agriculture industries for 10 years after her employment ends. Claire quits to work for AgriCo, a corporate farming concern. Can Tchotschky's prevent her employment with a court order?

5. Same as above, but Claire goes to work for Willie McFun's Restaurant as a marketing executive. Can Tchotschky's recover?

6. Maria is an electrical engineer who designs cutting-edge memory chips for Advanced Microtel Semiconductor Corp. in Farapolis, Minnekota. She has a non-compete agreement with AMS that prohibits her from doing memory-chip design for two years for other employers anywhere in the world, not just in Minnekota. Is the agreement enforceable?

7. WTBDWY (What's The Big Deal With Yogurt?) employs Betty in their store in the mall to mix the ingredients to make the yogurt. Betty quits to go to Lucy's Ice Cream to make yogurt for them. Can WTBDWY get a court order to prevent Betty from divulging its yogurt recipes?

8. Advanced Microtel Semiconductor Corp.'s contract with Maria provides that the general electrical-engineering know-how she picks up on the job will be a trade secret of AMS's. Is the contract enforceable?

9. As chief of food operations, Hirotaka knows the trade-secret recipe of Tennesouri Fried Chicken. He quits and starts Missouressee Fried Chicken. Hirotaka hires Catherine, a renowned taster and chef, to eat TFC food and perform chemical analysis and experimental cooking to figure out the secret TFC recipe. Can TFC enjoin these operations?

10. Advanced Microtel Semiconductor Corp. required Charlie, a cafeteria worker, to sign a contract assigning all inventions to AMS. Charlie invented a solar-heated ice-cream scooper in his garage and patented it. Is it property of AMS?

11. Lisa is an editor of *For the Love of Earth* magazine. In her off time, she writes an article about global warming. Does the copyright belong to the magazine?

IV. Privacy, Expression, and Affiliation Rights

1. Betty abducted Winthrop from a nearby accounting firm and imprisoned him in her basement to do her highly complicated tax returns. By smuggling papers to his attorney through the laundry vent, Winthrop sues Betty, claiming that she has violated his constitutional rights. Betty counters that since she is not an agent of the government, there is no state action to sustain a constitutional claim. Who's correct?

2. When Democratic president Clint Bilton took office, he went around the White House shaking hands and making small talk with the staff. He was shocked to discover that the employees of the travel office—all hired by the previous administration—were all conservative Republicans. Clint had them fired the next day. Do the travel-office employees have a claim?

3. When Billie Mae Hutchins, the U.S. secretary of education, decided to run for the U.S. Senate, she hired the assistant secretary of education to be the chairman of her campaign. Were any laws been broken?

4. Rick, a postal counter clerk in Los Angeles, often tells customers that the post office is a government monopoly designed to keep track of citizens so the government can control their minds. Frightened customers sometimes leave, saying they'll take their packages to UPS. After repeated warnings, the post-office supervisor fires Rick because of his remarks. Have Rick's First Amendment rights been violated?

5. Carlos, the assistant to the U.S. ambassador to Botsbabwe, lives in an apartment on the U.S. embassy grounds and drives a government-owned Plymouth. One night FBI agents break into his apartment and car and search them as part of a new program of

President George Shush to "get tough on drugs." Have Carlos's rights under the Fourth Amendment been violated?

6. Julie is employed as an accountant in the back office of Castaway Brewery. Her boss, Hans, tells her that she is to attend a rally after work to push passage of the Enlightened Youth Beer Act, which would lower the drinking age for beer to 18. Julie does not agree with the act, declines to attend, and is fired. Does she have a claim?

7. Scott and Anu are bottle-cap checkers at Castaway Brewery. Angry about Julie's dismissal, Scott goes to the vice president and tells him how unfair the firing was, and Anu delivers a short speech in the cafeteria to the other workers about how outraged they ought to be at such injustice in the workplace. Both Scott and Anu are fired. Do they have claims?

8. Gary repairs cars for Zanwark Garage. Beverly, the garage manager, was under the impression that one of the workers had stolen fuel injector nozzles, so she used a slim jim to open Gary's car—which was parked on garage property—and searched the glove compartment. Can Gary sue?

9. Gordon is a financial analyst with Bull Brothers Investment Bank. Gordon's boss, Ellen, hears that Gordon is gay. Curious to find out if the rumor is true, she has the maintenance staff install a jumper on the telephone switchboard that will allow her to listen in on his phone conversations. Does Gordon have a claim against Ellen under federal law?

10. A year later, Bull Bros. begins an internal investigation on the suspicion that some employees may have embezzled money from bank clients. The bank tells Gordon he must undergo a lie detector test as part of the investigation. Does Gordon have a claim against Bull Bros.?

11. Having finally had it, Gordon quits Bull Bros. and starts searching for other work. Ellen, while playing poker with many of the city's other bank higher-ups, decides to spill some gossip about Gordon: "I had this employee who's as gay you've ever seen! Of course, *I* am not uncomfortable with that, but he flirted with straight male clients during presentations, and that's just bad for business." In fact, Gordon has never had any contact with bank clients, much less flirted with them. Does Gordon have a claim for defamation?

V. DISCRIMINATION

1. Is "female Jew" a status or class?

2. What are the three models of discrimination?

3. The Good Ol' Boys, a country music group of all white males, refuses to hire George, a steel guitar player. George taped a telephone conversation with the Good Ol' Boys in which they say that the reason they didn't hire him is because he is black. What model of discrimination would George use in a Title VII suit?

4. Roslyn, a black woman, alleges in her Title VII complaint that Taco Land, a Mexican fast-food restaurant, declined to hire her for a cashier position and later hired Juanita, a Hispanic woman, for the job. The defendant Taco Land denies that it declined to hire

Roslyn because of her race, and answers that the reason she was not hired was that she had only one year of cashier experience, not the two years required. A private investigator for the Roslyn finds out that Juanita had no cashier experience at all and even told this to Taco Land during her interview. Is Roslyn now entitled to summary judgment?

5. Mauler Auto Wreckers declines to hire Jonathon, an Orthodox Jew, as an auto-compactor operator. A private investigator tapes a conversation with Nate, the manager, in which Nate says he didn't hire Jonathon both because he had a college degree—and therefore seemed overqualified for the job—*and* because Nate hates Jews. Using this evidence, can Jonathon establish a violation of Title VII?

6. Jack Rabbit Cab Co. is a local taxicab company in Vista Bonita, a town where 78 percent of the population is ethnic Vietnamese, 13 percent is ethnic Chinese, 6 percent is white, and 3 percent of the population is black. Jack Rabbit has 121 white cab drives, 7 black cab drivers, 9 other employees, all of whom are white, and no employees at all of Southeast Asian ancestry. Can a Title VII violation be established for discrimination against persons of Vietnamese ancestry? And if so, under what specific theory?

7. The O'Donnell Consulting Group provides management consulting services to a variety of Fortune 500 companies all over the world. In keeping with their image as a firm of winning, energized consultants, O'Donnell requires consulting candidates to be able to do five consecutive overhand chin-ups. Jessica, a law-school grad turned down for the job, found out that of the 25 women they interviewed on campus, five passed the chin-up test, and of the 50 men they interviewed, 20 men passed. Should Jessica be able to interest the EEOC in prosecuting a case against O'Donnell?

8. Ice Scraper, an up-and-coming black rap artist, hired Hannah, a white female, to sing back-up on his album. When it came time for Ice Scraper to go on tour, he told Hannah that he wouldn't hire her for the tour; he just couldn't have a white woman singing back up on stage. The rest of the band, after all, was black, he said, and they were playing black music to a black audience. Does Hannah have a claim under federal law?

9. Hannah calls a lawyer the same night Ice Scraper delivers the bad news, and she tells the lawyer that she wants to file suit in federal court the very next day. What should the lawyer advise her?

10. Thu, a Vietnamese immigrant in Vista Bonita, is starting a new cab company. Because of the Jack Rabbit Cab Co.'s failure to hire any Vietnamese, Thu says on the Vista Bonita Eyewitness News that Thu's Cab Co. will hire only ethnic Vietnamese persons. Thu buys four cabs and, as promised, his first 10 employees are all ethnic Vietnamese. Has Thu violated Title VII?

11. Rodney is an employee of Valerie's Whisper, a chain of lingerie shops. Rodney is the only male employee in the mall store, and the women clerks who work there occasionally slap him on the butt, grab his genitals through his pants, and tease him that he works there only so he can get a discount on thong underwear. When Paula, the supervisor, sees Jenny doing this to Rodney, she disciplines Jenny and tells other clerks that they cannot engage in such behavior. She tells Rodney if it happens again, he should notify her immediately so she can review security tapes and fire the employee

responsible. Rodney, however, feels he has had enough. He initiates action under Title VII for sexual harassment. Does he have a claim?

12. Valerie's Whisper fires Bonnie, a clerk, when a supervisor learns that she has gotten pregnant. Does Bonnie have a claim for sexual discrimination under Title VII?

13. Castaway Brewery refuses to hire non-citizens. Sundar, a non-citizen born in India, is refused a job. Can he prevail in a suit under Title VII?

14. Same as the previous, but Castaway Brewery is located in El Paso, Texas, a place with a large legal-alien Hispanic population. Castaway Brewery's proprietor, R.C., is known to dislike Hispanics. Can Sundar prevail in a Title VII suit?

15. At the small law firm of Blankenhap, Steadley & Winthrump, there are eight secretaries, all of whom are female, and nine paralegals, of whom eight are male and one is a female. Because of the way the firm culture has developed, the secretaries spend about half their time doing cite checking, file creation, organizing discovery documents, and other kinds of paralegal-type work. The paralegals themselves spend a large part of the day doing secretarial work, including entering corrections, answering phones, and getting coffee for the partners. Secretaries are paid and average of $29,000 per year, and paralegals get an average of $38,000 per year. Do the secretaries have a claim under the EPA?

16. Holly applies for a job as a test pilot with Sparrow Aerospace. She is rejected because her thighs—measured by the crux of the knee to the hip bone—are only 14 inches long. Sparrow requires test pilots to have thighs of at least 14.5 inches because of the contours of its ejection seats. Holly asks if Sparrow could modify the ejection seats to accommodate her thighs. The chief of flight test operations tells Holly that the seats could be easily and inexpensively modified, but standards are standards, and they will not hire her. Does Holly have a claim under the ADA?

17. Because of limited function in his legs, Mitch cannot walk without the assistance of crutches, and he cannot drive a car without a special hand lever that operates the brakes. Mitch applies for a job as a driver with Jack Rabbit Cab Co. Assuming Mitch is otherwise the best person for the job, must Jack Rabbit install a hand lever on one of its cabs so that Mitch can drive it?

VI. Wages and Hours

1. Brandon is a professional disc jockey who makes a $10,000 annual salary at K-Soft 101.1 FM. He does the overnight shift, from midnight to 5:30 a.m., six days a week. He receives a computer-generated log sheet of all the music he is to play, and the station provides several index cards with announcements and key phrases Brandon must use on the air, such as "K-Soft, the music of your life." After his airshift, Brandon must also dub commercials from reel-to-reel tape into the audio-playback computer, which takes him an average of two-and-a-half hours each day. To what monetary award, if any, is Brandon entitled under the FLSA?

2. K-Soft changes its format and becomes "X-Radio," touting the slogan, "The Audio Experiment." Chuck, the new program director, tells Brandon that he doesn't need a

silly computer-generated printout to tell him what to play or ridiculous index cards to tell him what to say. Therefore, Chuck says, Brandon is not to use his own good judgment and creative tastes in deciding what to play and what to say on the air. As the disc jockeys watch the index cards burn in a ceremonial fire in the parking lot, Chuck announces that, unfortunately, salary and off-air duties will stay the same for all on-air personalities. To what monetary award, if any, is Brandon entitled under the FLSA?

3. Molly works for Paintdrying.com, an internet start-up that allows people—for only 99 cents a minute—to see live pictures of actual paint that is in the process of drying. Molly is vice president of marketing, which means that she, like most others there, spends the majority of her time writing programming code according to the specific instructions of Connie, the CEO. In addition to Connie and Molly, there are four other employees of Paintdrying.com, all of whom are vice presidents of something-or-other. Because Paintdrying.com has yet to turn a profit, Molly and the other VPs are all paid primarily with stock options and therefore have to live with their parents. The only cash that employees receive is a $3 per hour "food and hygiene allowance." Can Molly recover from Paintdrying.com under the FLSA?

4. Janet is employed by the government of Lee County as the night magistrate. She is paid $5 for each search warrant she issues, and nothing for applications she denies. Janet, who is trying to support a family, works hard at finding probable cause wherever she can, issuing between 10 and 15 warrants over a typical eight-hour shift. Is Lee County liable under the FLSA?

5. Karen hires Phoebe, a plumber, to install new pipe under the sink in her home. Karen says times are tough, and she will only pay Phoebe $10 for the three hours of work. Can Phoebe recover under the FLSA?

6. Valley View Drug Store fires Katie, a senior at the University of Nevaho, and hires in her place Josh, a student at nearby Central High School. Josh earns $4.25 and hour from May 21st, the first day of summer vacation to the last day, September 6th. Is Valley View Drug Store liable?

7. When the town of Valley View hosts the Jet Dragster Nationals competition, Josh works a 50-hour week to keep the drug store stocked with aspirin and Tylenol for spectators coming back from the raceway, a mere 200 yards away. Instead of paying Josh time-and-a-half for the extra 10 hours, Valley View Drug Store gives him the next two weeks off as paid vacation and presents him with the keys to the spacious and peaceful company retreat at Lake Sierra. Is the drug store liable under the FLSA?

8. Jeff is the junior engineer for X-Radio, which has an old transmitter and unreliable studio equipment that could break down at any time. Every other week Jeff is on call, meaning he must keep his pager on and cannot go more than 15 miles away from the studio. Is Jeff owed the minimum wage for his on-call time?

9. Dangerous Dave, X-Radio's star afternoon personality, slams his fist so hard on the studio control panel that he keeps breaking the buttons, making the controls inoperable. Eager to keep Dangerous Dave happy and on the air, the program director has Jeff stay at the station an extra hour after his work is done and watch TV, read books, or do whatever else in the conference room while Dangerous Dave is on the air, just in case Jeff is needed for a quick repair. Must X-Radio pay Jeff for this time?

10. When the transmitter at X-Radio suddenly broke down last Thursday, Jeff had to leave home at 8 p.m. to drive to the studio. At 9 p.m., he got to the studio and hopped into the engineering truck, which he drove to the transmitter site at the top of Rose Peak. He got to the transmitter at 10 p.m., spent two hours fixing it, and got back to the studio at 1 a.m. Getting back into his car, it took him another hour to drive home. How many hours should Jeff put down on his time sheet?

11. Next Monday, instead of reporting to the studio for work, Jeff is told to go to the transmitter site where he will work all day doing regular maintenance. Jeff has to get the engineering truck at the studio first, but the general manager tells him not to clock in until he gets to the top of Rose Peak, since he will spend the entire workday there. When may Jeff clock in?

12. Josh, the high school student working over the summer at Valley View Drug Store, learns that one of his girlfriends from last semester, Allison, has just had his baby. Josh wants to take unpaid leave under the Family and Medical Leave Act. Is he so entitled?

13. Allison has worked as the reporter covering the education beat for the Valley View Gazette full-time for the past three years. When she has her baby, she calls up the Gazette and tells her editor that she will be taking the next 12 weeks off as unpaid leave under the FMLA. Can the Gazette fire her for doing so?

14. Allison's editor says that he will gladly allow her to take her leave starting immediately. But when Allison returns to the Gazette three months later, her editor informs her that they have hired an education reporter in her place during her absence. They will give her a position as the legal beat reporter at the same pay and benefits. Can Allison sue the Gazette for not holding her old position open for her?

VII. BENEFITS

1. Advanced Hair Technologies, Inc. builds a line of high-end blow dryers and electric curlers. AHT offers a program to its electrical engineers where it will pay $500 every month into special retirement accounts earmarked for the individual employees. The employees will get a choice of mutual funds into which they may direct that their funds be invested. What kind of pension plan does AMS have?

2. Theo, the chief financial officer of AHT, is also the plan fiduciary of a defined-benefit plan that AHT offers to its factory workers. The pension fund holds 20 percent of the outstanding stock in AHT. Theo overhears a conversation at the opera that its competitor, AeroBlow, is about to offer a new blowdryer—the MegaBlow Plus. The MegaBlow Plus will be much more advanced than AHT's top-of-the-line DevilBreath 2000, and it will be sold for half the cost. Theo knows this will eventually cause AHT's stock value to drop, but if he sells the pension plan stock, he will flood the market, start a panic, and accelerate the devaluation of AHT's stock. What should Theo do?

3. Samantha is about to retire from AHT. Under the terms of the pension plan, Samantha is not entitled to any pension plan benefits if she retires before 60. AHT is suffering declining profit margins, so in order to save some expenses, just days before her 60th birthday, AHT fires Samantha. Does Samantha have a claim against AHT?

4. The state of New Merizona passes a law stating that anytime a round of layoffs follows a corporate merger, all the employees laid off must be given a stipend for job retraining. Is the law preempted?

5. TransOceanic Air gives all flight-attendant candidates a brochure about what their benefits will be if they join the company. The brochure says that TransOceanic has secured deals with 11 major airlines around the world such that retired TransOceanic flight attendants will be able to fly standby for only $15 to most major destinations in Europe and the Americas. In fact, TransOceanic never made any such deals with other airlines. Can the flight attendants sue in tort for fraud?

6. Harriet, a TransOceanic baggage handler, contracted type-III craniomyoloma, a fast-moving cancer that is highly treatable if caught in time. Under TransOceanic's health-benefits policy, Harriet must get approval from her physician and a cost-management review officer at TransCare—TransOceanic's designated HMO—before any cancer-treatment payments can be approved. Although Harriet got the physician approval, the cost-management review officer, in an effort to increase his end-of-the-year bonus, delayed approval for months. Two days after the approval was put into the mail, Harriet died. Can Harriet's survivors sue for wrongful death?

7. If Harriet's survivors sue under ERISA, what may they recover?

8. New Merizona passes the HIV Rights Act, a law which requires that all health insurance plans must cover AIDS and HIV-related illnesses for up to $500,000 per person. Is the law preempted by ERISA?

9. First New Merizona Bank does not buy health insurance for its employees from an outside vendor, but instead has created a fund that it uses to pay employee health-care costs. Jane is a teller at the bank who is HIV-positive. The bank's plan caps coverage for AIDS and HIV-related illnesses at $10,000 per person. Does ERISA preempt the HIV Rights Act (discussed in the previous question) insofar as it would allow employees with HIV to sue the bank for additional coverage?

10. Jane's son Roberto has always been covered by his mother's health plan. When he graduates from high school, he decides he will surf in Hawaii for a year before enrolling at Stalevard College. A month after he graduates he turns 18, and his coverage under Jane's health plan terminates. There are 11 months to go before he can get on the student health-plan at college. Can Roberto use COBRA to fill the gap?

11. Heather is self-employed freelance translator and had not had health insurance for three months when she enrolled as an individual in SemiCare, an HMO plan. SemiCare notifies her that it will not cover her for arthritis, because it is a pre-existing condition. Six months later, Heather gets a job with HalfwayHealth, an HMO that provides her with membership in its own plan as a benefit. Heather then terminates the SemiCare plan. Seven months after later, Heather's arthritis-condition acts up and she needs to see physician. HalfwayHealth says that the arthritis is excluded from coverage as a pre-existing condition. Can HalfwayHealth get away with this?

12. During his year of surfing, Roberto becomes very grateful for having made his COBRA election—he's been treated for shark bites three times. But when next summer rolls around, he still doesn't want to go to school. Tired of sharks, Roberto decides to spend the next year snowboarding in Colorado and Chile. He tells Stalevard that he's not coming, and he applies for SemiCare's individual plan. Although he meets the eligibility requirements of the plan, SemiCare denies Roberto's application. Can SemiCare get away with this?

VIII. OSHA

1. Advanced Hair Technologies, Inc. operates a metal-injection molder, the Volcano 300, for making parts for its electric curlers. The molder is unique in the curler manufacturing industry. After casting a part, the Volcano 300 opens for only two seconds, during which an employee must reach into it with asbestos gloves and pull out the part. The molder then automatically closes and molten metal is injected. Nine times in the past three months, employee's hands have been caught in the molder. Based on the above, is AHT in violation of the general-duty clause?

2. Can Nina, an employee injured by AHT's Volcano 300, sue under OSHA?

3. The Volcano 300 has accumulated a bad reputation in the industry since the accidents at AHT. ScalpStyle, a new curler manufacturer, is unfamiliar with the Volcano 300's infamous record, however. ScalpStyle purchases a Volcano 300 and begins manufacturing operations. As soon as one employee is injured, the company discontinues use of the machine. Has ScalpStyle violated OSHA?

4. Jeff, an engineer for X-Radio, must occasionally climb to the top of the transmitter tower to change the light bulbs. (The lights are required by the FAA for aviation safety.) X-Radio has supplied the normal compliment of climbing equipment, but repairing the transmitter is still quite dangerous. The station could make transmitter maintenance safer by installing a 200-foot-high staircase next to the transmitter tower. Does OSHA require X-Radio install the staircase?

5. After reviewing the X-Radio engineering department, an OSHA official issues an order to X-Radio. The order requires X-Radio to provide Jeff with pants padded in the buttocks with inch-thick polyurethane foam to protect him in the case of a fall from the tower. How should X-Radio contest the order?

6. For an extra $300, X-Radio could buy long-lasting light bulbs for the tower. With the long-lasting bulbs, Jeff would need to climb the tower only once every three years instead of every couple of months, as he does now. X-Radio admits this would massively decrease the chances of a fatal accident, but it's cheaper to have Jeff change the regular bulbs every couple of months. Must X-Radio buy the expensive long-lasting bulbs?

7. Ye Olde Sawmill is an authentic old New England sawmill with large plexiglass windows where tourists, for a fee, can watch "lumber processing *as it used to be*." An OSHA standard promulgated under § 6(a) prescribes that all electric- or gas-powered circular saws with blades over 12 inches in diameter must have safety guards on them.

Ye Olde Sawmill operates a 60-inch blade circular saw. Because the saw is powered by a water wheel, the OSHA standard does not require a blade guard. The secretary of labor orders that the words "electric- or gas-powered" be stricken from the standard so that all circular saws will be covered. Must Ye Olde Sawmill comply with the modified language?

8. The secretary of labor seeks to adopt a new standard under § 6(b) that would require a flashing red light atop water-powered circular saws to warn nearby persons before the saw is started. The secretary issues a report concluding: "There is a risk, although extremely minor, that without the warning light, persons will be dangerously close to the saw when it is re-engaged with the water-wheel transmission." Will the rule survive a challenge by Ye Olde Sawmill?

9. Next door to the sawmill is Ye Olde Souvenir Shoppe, a small operation that makes varnished-wood paperweights and refrigerator magnets. The secretary of labor introduces a new prospective standard, to be promulgated under § 6(b), to deal with the substantial cancer risk posed by inhalation of varnish fumes. The new standard prescribes a specific maximum exposure to the varnish fumes and requires workers to be supplied with lapel-pin spectrometers, which would measure the varnish exposure. Compliance would drive Ye Olde Souvenir Shoppe out of business, since it would have to buy the lapel-pin spectrometers, reconfigure the workshop, and install an industrial ventilation system with chemical air scrubbers. Can Ye Olde Souvenir Shoppe successfully challenge the standard?

10. Ye Olde Sawmill requires employees on the mill floor to wear costumes with big, floppy shoes. The shoes make it easy to trip and fall into the whirling blades. Tony, a mill-floor employee, complains about the condition to OSHA. Ye Olde Sawmill fires Tony "for being a crybaby and going off to the feds." Can Tony sue Ye Olde Sawmill under OSHA?

11. In the booming economy, Ye Olde Sawmill has trouble hiring people who want to dress in old-fashioned costumes and work in a sawmill. But they succeed in hiring Arto, a hyperactive 20-year-old. Within weeks, Arto is teaching other employees "lumber surfing," a game where they stand atop lumber moving on the conveyer belt and then jump off just before it is sucked into the spinning blades. Sean, the floor supervisor, tells Arto to cut it out and to tell the other workers that it's dangerous and they shouldn't do it. Felix, an impressionable 18-year-old, subsequently tries the game and loses a foot. Ye Olde Sawmill contests the assessment of OSHA fines arguing that the employees were not complying with workplace rules forbidding lumber surfing, and therefore the mill is not to blame for the injury. Can Ye Olde Sawmill avoid liability?

IX. WORKERS' COMPENSATION

1. Elmer operates a dragline—a large machine that digs ditches—for the Great Lakes & Minniana Railway. One day a cable snaps and Elmer's arm is badly broken. The dragline that GL&M Railway was operating was the safest dragline on the market, and they had taken pains to make sure the dragline had undergone regular maintenance.

Assuming Elmer cannot show that the GL&M Railway has been negligent, can he still recover workers' compensation benefits?

2. Elmer later discovers that the GL&M Railway failed to replace the dragline cables as recommended by the manufacturer. Can Elmer prevail in a tort suit against the railroad?

3. Joey works at Old Banana, a clothing store in the mall. The music played over the PA system in Old Banana is on a tape loop that repeats every 30 minutes. After hearing "Day-O" for the 43rd time over a busy Labor Day weekend, Joey has a mental breakdown. After the episode, he bursts into tears every time he sees neatly folded clothing. Subsequently, Joey is unable to work for the next two weeks. Is he entitled to workers' comp benefits?

4. When Joey returns to work at Old Banana, the tape is different, but it still repeats every half-hour. Over the course of three days, Joey hears "Lady in Red" 73 times. On hearing it the 73rd time, he runs screaming to the back of the store and slams his head in one of the fitting-room doors upwards of 30 times. Is treatment for Joey's subsequent concussion covered by workers' comp?

5. To encourage camaraderie, Zippo's, a copy store, invites employees to a party after the store closes with free drinks and mini-pizza-bagels. Activities include several contests, such as speed stapling and rubberband archery. During a race to see who can collate the fastest, Amanda suffers a severe paper cut that requires stitches. Is Amanda covered by workers' comp?

6. Cathleen and Mack, two disc jockeys at X-Radio, are hanging out in the music director's office after hours. Finding a stack of discarded compacts discs, Cathleen and Mack decide to test exactly how indestructible CDs actually are. They microwave one, drop another from a second-story window, and then they each take one and bend it backwards as far as possible. Cathleen's CD snaps and she ends up driving a two-inch shard through her palm. Mack's CD splinters and a sharp piece flies into the air and hits the eyeball of Paul, another disc jockey who was walking by. Is Cathleen's injury compensable? Is Paul's?

7. A couple weeks later, Dangerous Dave, before doing his nighttime airshift, blows out his voice recording a monster-truck commercial. Since Dangerous Dave cannot now get on the air, the program director calls Paul and asks him to come back to work to do Dangerous's shift. On the way over, Paul's car is hit by a CitiScurry bus, and Paul is injured. Is Paul covered by workers' comp?

8. While driving back to town after covering the 98-SyncBoyz concert, Cathleen decides to take a detour to the Summit Hotel & Casino to play a few hands of poker. Inside the casino, she is grazed by a bullet during a casino heist. Is her injury covered by workers' comp?

9a. Martha is a reporter for the Valley View Gazette. On the crimes beat, she spends a good part of her day in her car going to crime scenes, police stations, and jails. One day, while driving to a crime scene, she is hit and injured by a drunk driver. Did her injury arise out of employment under the proximate-cause doctrine?

9b. Under the peculiar-risk doctrine?

9c. Under the increased-risk doctrine?

9d. Under the actual-risk doctrine?

9e. Under the positional-risk doctrine?

10. Which of the following is most likely not to be based on lost earnings capacity: temporary partial disability, temporary total disability, permanent partial disability, or permanent total disability?

11. Mario, the proprietor of the Ziff Cafe, is sick and tired of Ricardo, his chief chef. So late one night Mario takes out a hammer and cracks the hose fitting for the gas supply to the range. When Ricardo comes into work the next day, he goes to ignite the range and is badly burned in a fireball caused by the escaped gas. Can Ricardo sue the Ziff Cafe and Mario in tort?

12. Traci is a waitress at the Ziff Cafe. After work she meets her boyfriend to have drinks at the bar. She badly cuts her lip on a broken glass. Can Traci sue the Ziff Cafe in tort?

X. UNEMPLOYMENT INSURANCE

1. Rachael quits her job as an operator at TeleLink Long Distance because her mother is very ill, and she needs to move back home to take care of her. Is Rachael eligible for unemployment-insurance benefits?

2. Beth is repair technician at TeleLink. She quits because, as the only female repair technician, she feels harassed. Other technicians often made comments about her breasts and whistled whenever she climbed a telephone pole. She is thinking about a Title VII suit, but in the meantime, can she get unemployment-insurance benefits?

3. Jack is one of the employees who made lewd comments to Beth, causing her to quit and launch accusations of sexual harassment against TeleLink. After finding out about Jack's participation in the matter, TeleLink fires him. Can Jack collect unemployment benefits?

4. Gerald was a member of the band Teenage Ritalin Riot—which had been getting regular gigs—before the leader threw a temper tantrum and disbanded the group. Gerald is now collecting unemployment. He tried to get a job with Third Blinking Goo Eye 20, but that band rejected him because his hair was too long and unkempt. May Gerald's unemployment benefits be cancelled for this?

5. Gerald declines a job offer from FrugalMax, a discount retailer that sells surplus and irregular clothing. May Gerald's unemployment benefits be cancelled because of his refusing the job?

REVIEW QUIZ ANSWERS

I. WHO IS AN EMPLOYEE?

1. **NO**—Because Eugene has substantial control over his work, he is an independent contractor under the common-law test. Additionally, the factors of the economic-realities test clearly indicate independent-contractor status.

2. **DEPENDS**—Because Eugene still controls the way in which the work is done during the specified hours, he would likely still be an independent contractor under the common-law test. The result under the economic-realities test is indefinite, however, since the control of the jobs is more divided between the employer and the employee, and unlike in the previous question, Eugene is not exposed to profit-and-loss variability since he takes a $6-an-hour wage.

3. **YES**—Although Kate gets a commission, and therefore shares in the profits, this alone does not turn a sales employee into a sales contractor. Notice that the employer seems to acquiesce to employee status, since it guarantees a minimum wage no matter how low commissions fall.

4. **DEPENDS**—Yes under the common law, no under the economic-realities test. Under the common law, Kate is an employee, because even though she controls much of the way in which she does the work, the employer still has the *right* to control the manner of work, and the common-law test is based on who has the "right to control." Under the economic-realities test, Kate is not an employee because factors such as control, profit-and-loss, capital investment, permanency, integral to hiring party's business, and dependence of the worker all militate in favor of finding an employment relationship.

5. **YES**—Under *Vizcaino v. Microsoft*, the contract signed by the parties is not controlling—courts look to the circumstances of the relationship.

II. DISCHARGE

1. **YES**—At-will is a two-way street. Both the employee as well as the employer have the right to terminate the employment relationship at any time

2. **BOB**—It does not matter that Arkassippi is an at-will state, because the at-will rule is only a default rule or presumption. As long as Bob can convince a jury that there was a contract, he will prevail.

3. **YES**—Goldie's quit would constitute "constructive discharge."

4. **PROBABLY**—in most jurisdictions, since the harassment would cause the reasonable employee to quit, the action would be constructive discharge. A minority of states, however, require that the intolerable conditions were created with the intent of making the employee quit.

5. **NO**—If the contract only specifies a duration, without more, then a just-cause standard is presumed. Firing an employee—who has done nothing wrong—to make room for another does not constitute just cause.

6. **MAYBE**—Jurisdictions are split as to whether adverse business conditions and management reorganization constitute just cause.

7. **MAYBE**—The question is whether the jurisdiction subscribes to the rate-of-pay rule. If so, then Jared had a contract for at least a month of employment, and he has a claim for breach.

8. **$1 MILLION**—The employee is liable for the difference between his contract salary and the salary required to hire a worker to replace him.

9. **NO**—The 13th Amendment has been interpreted to prohibit injunctions that compel an individual to work.

10. **NO**—Jaime has a duty to mitigate damages by looking for other comparable work. If he finds other work at a lower wage, he may recover the difference in wages.

11. **$33,000**—Jutta may recover all of her wage from her six months of unemployment ($15,000), but for the remaining year on the contract ($30,000), she must deduct any salary earned at the yogurt store ($12,000), even if the job is not similar to her old employment. For the second year, $30,000 – $12,000 = $18,000. That plus $15,000 lost salary in the first year adds up to $33,000.

12. **NO**—While some jurisdictions vary on how large a disclaimer must be, a very prominent one would easily prevent the manual from forming a contract.

13. **YES**—Alisa can recover if she can establish that there was a binding oral contract that included the job security provision. If something prevented such a finding, however, she could sue under a theory of promissory estoppel, since she took the job in reasonable reliance on the promise of job security.

14. **MAYBE**—Although jurisdictions differ, the statutory and constitutional right to vote could well give rise to a cause of action in tort for wrongful discharge in violation of public policy.

15. **MAYBE**—While it depends on the jurisdiction, Gretchen's whistleblowing may be protected by a whistleblower statute, or could be actionable under the tort of WDVPP, since protecting the public's health in an important public policy.

16. **NO**—On these facts alone, there is no claim. WARN is only applicable to firms with 100 or more employees.

17. **NO**—The Lloyd-LaFollete Act of 1912 prohibits discharge of civil servants unless it is in the interests of the efficiency of the service. Because Kit's discharge was for political reasons, it fails the statutory standard. Here, we have the additional evidence that her discharge was actually *because of* her superior efficiency, making the outcome doubly clear.

18. **YES**—Laura's tenure establishes a property right to her job. Thus, she is entitled to procedural due process before she can be fired. At a minimum, she must have notice of the charges and an opportunity to be heard.

III. EMPLOYEE DUTIES AND OBLIGATIONS

1. **YES**—Jim has not acted for the benefit of the employer in all matters connected with his employment, so under the Restatement, he has breached his duty of loyalty.

2. **NO**—While it is a breach of the duty of loyalty to solicit customers, merely informing them of future plans is generally not considered a breach.

3. **YES**—Under the corporate-opportunities doctrine, Florence must give the opportunity over to Livingston, because it is clearly within Livingston's line of business.

4. **NO**—The non-compete agreement here is not reasonable in scope or duration. AgriCo is not in competition with Tchotschky's, and no legitimate interest of Tchotschky's is served by preventing Claire's employment at AgriCo.

5. **DEPENDS**—Willie McFun's sounds like a direct competitor to Tchotschky's, but the covenant must serve legitimate interests beyond preventing a competitor from hiring a former employee. If Tchotschky's can show that as a chef, Claire had access to trade secrets that she would likely exploit as a marketing executive for Willie McFun's, then Tchotschky's may be able to take some legal action. Regardless of what Tchotschky's can show, however, 10 years is an unreasonably long time for the restriction to persist.

6. **YES**—On these facts alone, the agreement is reasonable and enforceable. Since a microchip manufacturer ordinarily has a global market, and not just a local one, the worldwide ban is reasonable.

7. **NO**—An injunction would only be appropriate if WTBDWY had protected their recipe as a trade secret. Here there is no indication that they did.

8. **NO**—General know-how is not protectible as a trade secret.

9. **NO**—Catherine's experimental work is reverse engineering, and reverse engineering is always an appropriate way of gaining access to another's trade secret.

10. **NO**—Most courts would refuse to enforce such an assignment clause insofar as it purports to extend to inventions that do not relate to the employer's business and inventions not developed at work.

11. **NO**—Even though Lisa is involved in the creation of copyrightable works as part of her job, if her global warming article was prepared during off hours, then it is her property, absent an agreement to the contrary.

IV. PRIVACY, EXPRESSION, AND AFFILIATION RIGHTS

1. **WINTHROP**—The 13th Amendment prohibits slavery and involuntary servitude, period. There is no state-action requirement for this constitutional prohibition.

2. **YES**—Federal employees cannot be hired or fired on the basis of political affiliation, unless they are in a high policy-making job. (The assistant secretary of transportation, for instance, may be fired by the new president.)

3. **YES**—The Hatch Act prohibits federal employees from running political campaigns and engaging in various other political activities.

4. **NO**—Under the *Pickering* three-part test, Rick's speech *was* on a matter of public concern and *was* a motivating factor in his discharge, but the government's interest in the efficient operation of the workplace outweighs Rick's interest in the speech as a citizen.

5. **YES**—The Fourth Amendment's prohibition of unreasonable searches and seizures applies to government-owned property where an employee has a reasonable and actual expectation of privacy. Under these facts, Carlos would have such an expectation in his car and home, and a policy of "getting tough on drugs" would not be sufficient to defeat this expectation of privacy.

6. **MAYBE**—Under cases such as *Novosel* and *Chavez*, Ellen would have a good claim for wrongful discharge in violation of public policy where the public policy is free expression. But these cases do not necessarily reflect the state of the law in most jurisdictions

7. **NO FOR SCOTT, YES FOR ANU**—Anu's communication with her other employees is speech related to concerted activity undertaken for mutual aid or protection. Because such action is the first step in unionizing, it is protected under the NLRA, whether it is designed to lead to eventual unionization or not. Scott's rant to the boss, however, is unprotected by the NLRA, because as a solo effort, it is not "concerted" activity.

8. **YES**—Gary can sue for the intrusion-upon-seclusion branch of the tort of wrongful invasion of privacy. Gary had a reasonable expectation of privacy in his car, and the invasion would be highly offensive to the reasonable person.

9. **YES TO BOTH**—This wiretap is in violation of the Omnibus Crime Control and Safe Streets Act of 1968. Listening in because of a curiosity about someone's sexual orientation does not qualify under the business exception.

10. **NO**—Provided certain procedural guidelines are followed, the bank may ask employees to submit to polygraph tests in the course of investigating a theft.

11. **MAYBE**—The only problem in constructing a defamation claim for Gordon is that it is not clear that Ellen identified Gordon to the other bankers. If mentioning that he recently quit her bank is enough for the other bankers to figure out who he is, then Gordon would have a good claim for defamation.

V. DISCRIMINATION

1. **CLASS**—A class is a description of a person's status. The class label "female" describes a person's gender status. The class label "Jew" describes a person's religious and/or ethnic status.

2. **DISPARATE TREATMENT, DISPARATE IMPACT, REASONABLE ACCOMMODATION**

3. **DISPARATE TREATMENT**—Direct evidence of discrimination allows a claim based on individual disparate treatment.

4. **NO**—The highly criticized *St. Mary*'s case held that even if the plaintiff can prove that the defendant's alleged non-discriminatory motive for not hiring the worker was in fact pretext, the defendant can still defeat the suit by showing that the real reason was not discriminatory.

5. **YES**—According to the Civil Rights Act of 1991, as long as an impermissible factor (here animus against a religious group) was one of the motives in a hiring decision, then a violation is established. If Mauler Auto Wreckers can show that Jonathon wouldn't have been hired even if he weren't Jewish, then Jonathon's remedies would be limited to costs, fees, and injunctive relief, but the violation would still be established.

6. **YES, AS SYSTEMIC DISPARATE TREATMENT**—Systemic disparate treatment can be established without direct evidence where there are stark statistical disparities. Here, the disparity is much greater than *Teamsters*, so at least as far as these facts go, the case would seem to be pretty clear-cut. Even if the difference weren't "stark," the plaintiffs could use standard-deviation analysis to scrutinize the disparity.

7. **YES**—If five of 25 women passed, then 20 percent of women passed. If 20 of 50 men passed, then 40 percent of men passed. Since women pass the test half as often as men do, and because half is less than four-fifths, the test fails the four-fifths test. Also, despite O'Donnell's explanation for the physical tests, they do not seem to be legitimate business necessity.

8. **YES**—Ice Scraper has engaged in racial discrimination in a hiring decision, and no defenses are available. The BFOQ defense is not available for race. An affirmative-action-plan defense is not available, because there is no remedial purpose here—Ice Scraper's band is otherwise all black. Remember also that Title VII does not make an exception for "reverse discrimination," action that adversely impacts a majority class.

9. **SUE UNDER SECTION 1981**—For a Title VII claim, the plaintiff must first exhaust administrative remedies, such as with the EEOC, before she may sue. But § 1981, which prohibits racial discrimination in the making of contracts, requires no administrative exhaustion, so she could sue immediately.

10. **NO**—Title VII only covers employers with 15 or more employees.

11. **PROBABLY NOT**—Rodney has been sexually harassed, but there are barriers to constructing a claim under Title VII. He has no claim against the individual women, since Title VII does not allow action against other employees. Whether Valerie's Whisper can be sued depends on whether it can be held vicariously liable for its employees' harassment. Here Valerie's Whisper can argue that the employees were acting outside the scope of their employment in harassing Rodney, and that the employer had a way of correcting the discrimination by disciplining employees, but Rodney had failed to avail himself of these measures.

12. **YES**—The Pregnancy Discrimination Act of 1979 provides that discrimination on the basis of pregnancy is discrimination because of sex under Title VII.

13. NO—Title VII's prohibition on national-origin discrimination does not prohibit discrimination based on citizenship status. On these facts there is no Title VII violation.

14. PROBABLY—Here there is strong evidence that R.C. is using citizenship-status as a pretext for national-origin discrimination, which has adversely affected Sundar.

15. YES—This looks like a pretty good case for an EPA violation. The titles of the positions are not controlling, what matters if the positions involved are substantially equal in terms of skill, effort, and responsibility with similar working conditions.

16. NO—Holly does not have a disability under these facts. First of all, having 14-inch thighs is not an "impairment," since such a thigh length is not outside the normal range. Secondly, working at a particular job is never a "major life activity."

17. YES—Mitch's condition is a disability because it is an impairment (outside the normal range) that substantially limits a major life activity (he requires crutches to walk and a special device to drive). Supplying the braking hand lever is a reasonable accommodation—it's an affirmative employer action that allows him to do the job. On these facts, there are no applicable defenses.

VI. WAGES AND HOURS

1. $7,851.20 PER YEAR OF WORK—Brandon works eight hours a day six days a week, which is 48 hours per week. With 52 weeks in a year, he is being paid $4.01 per hour, which is well below the minimum wage. Brandon must be paid minimum wage ($5.15) for the first 40 hours of each week and 1.5 times minimum wage for the next eight hours. That adds up to $13,925.20. Brandon gets the difference between that and his paid salary plus an equal amount in liquidated damages. $13,925.60 – $10,000 = $3,925.60. $3,925.60 × 2 = $7,851.20. Even though Brandon is a "professional" disc jockey, his job does not pass the test for the white-collar exemption for professionals because he does not have a wide degree of latitude in using creativity and independent thinking in deciding how to do his work.

2. NONE—Through his liberal programming philosophy, Chuck has given Brandon a wide degree of latitude in using creativity and independent thinking in deciding how to do his work. Brandon might have an argument that his off-air work is not "professional," but his primary on-air work is.

3. YES—Molly is being paid less than minimum wage, and her job does not qualify for any white-collar exemption. She is not an "executive" because she does not supervise any other employees. She is not a "professional" because there is nothing to indicate that she has any degree of latitude in what she does or that she has minimal supervision. She is not an "administrator" because she does not exercise discretion and independent judgment.

4. NO—As long as Janet is actually being paid minimum wage, it does not matter that she is being paid a piece rate. The bottom range of her production is 10 warrants per eight hours, which is $6.25 per hour, which is above the $5.15 minimum. (Although okay under the FLSA, Lee County's clever scheme for incentivizing the issuance of search warrants is definitely a Fourth Amendment violation, so Janet's piece-rate days are numbered.)

5. **NO**—Phoebe is an independent contractor. The FLSA only applies to employees. (For the difference between independent contractors and employees, see Chapter I.)

6. **YES, TWO WAYS**—The drug store has violated the minimum wage provision, because the $4.25 subminimum youth-training wage is permitted for a maximum of 90-days. Additionally, firing Katie was a violation because employers may not fire regular employees to replace them with subminimum-wage workers.

7. **YES**—No matter how much Josh would rather have the cabin and the paid time-off, fringe benefits cannot offset overtime pay. The drug store is liable.

8. **NO**—This case is similar to *Bright*. Although Jeff might have to return to work at any moment, this on-call time can be used substantially for his own purposes and therefore need not be compensated.

9. **PROBABLY**—Waiting time at the workplace is usually compensable. Exceptions may be made when the waiting time is permissive enough that it may be used substantially for the employee's own benefit. This hour "after work" that he is required to stay in the conference room, however, is not likely to be permissive enough.

10. **SIX HOURS**—Because Jeff is coming back to work for an emergency, the commute from his home to work and back again is compensable.

11. **WHEN HE GETS TO THE STUDIO**—While commuting from home is not ordinarily compensable time, traveling between jobsites is, and the studio is a jobsite. Additionally, driving the engineering truck is a principle part of the job Jeff must do in doing maintenance on the transmitter, so that travel time is compensable.

12. **NO**—To be entitled to take leave under the FMLA, an employee must work for the present employer for 12 months. Josh was only working there for the summer.

13. **YES**—Wherever the reason for taking leave is foreseeable, the employee must give the employer 30 days notice. If Allison takes the leave without giving notice, she can be fired.

14. **NO**—The FMLA does not require the employer to restore the employee to the exact same position if the employer gives her an equivalent position with the same benefits and pay, subject to the same terms and conditions.

VII. BENEFITS

1. **DEFINED CONTRIBUTION PLAN**—In a defined benefit plan, the company guarantees a certain income during retirement. In a defined contribution plan, the company guarantees only the amount they will put into the plan at the outset.

2. **GET OUTSIDE INDEPENDENT COUNSEL**—While it is acceptable for Theo to be a plan fiduciary, when a conflict of interest arises, he should obtain outside, independent counsel and, if necessary, he should temporarily suspend his work as a fiduciary.

3. **YES**—This is a classic violation of ERISA § 510.

4. **NO**—This law does not regulate benefit "plans." The one-time payment to laid-off workers does not count as a plan for the purpose of ERISA preemption.

5. **NO**—ERISA preempts the use of all laws of general applicability insofar as they relate to an employee-benefit plan.

6. **NO**—TransCare is an ERISA fiduciary, and its actions in failing to provide benefits are not actionable under state law, because such laws are preempted by ERISA as they relate to the administration of employee-benefit plans.

7. **THE VALUE OF THE CANCER TREATMENT**—If a court determines that the cost-control management officer violated ERISA § 404 *[§ 1103]*[*], then § 502 *[§ 1132]* allows recovery of the value of the benefits wrongfully denied. Harriet's family is not entitled to punitive damages or compensatory damages for pain, suffering, loss of consortium, etc.

8. **NO**—Under ERISA's Insurance/Savings Clause, states are permitted to regulate the insurance industry.

9. **YES**—The Deemer Clause provides that if an employer self-insures, then that program will not be considered insurance for the purposes of the Insurance/Savings Clause. Therefore, the law is not saved from ERISA preemption.

10. **YES**—Roberto has 60 days from a qualifying event to elect COBRA coverage. Termination of coverage of a dependent because that dependent becomes too old for coverage counts as a qualifying event.

11. **NO**—HIPAA prohibits group health plans from excluding coverage for pre-existing conditions for a maximum of 12 months, and this period must be reduced by any period of creditable coverage. Heather's coverage under SemiCare's plan counts as six months of creditable coverage, so HalfwayHealth can exclude Heather's arthritis for only six months. At seven months, Heather is entitled to coverage.

12. **NO**—HIPAA provides that if an insurer sells health coverage to individuals, then that insurer cannot deny coverage to eligible persons who have been covered under a group health plan for 18 months.

VIII. OSHA

1. **YES**—OSHA requires that a workplace be free from recognized hazards that are likely to cause serious physical injury. The prior accidents establish The Volcano 300 to be recognized in the industry as dangerous, and therefore it is objectively recognized as a hazard.

2. **NO**—OSHA does not provide a private cause of action. Only the government can sue under OSHA.

3. **YES**—To be a recognized hazard, the hazard must meet *either* the subjective or the objective test. If the Volcano 300 is known in the industry to be dangerous, it does not

---

[*] Primary section references are to the ERISA act, bracketed references are to the codified section numbering scheme at 29 U.S.C.

matter whether ScalpStyle has actual knowledge—the hazard is objectively recognized.

4. **NO**—OSHA permits hazards that are not feasibly preventable. A remedial measure is unfeasible if it involves terrific cost, as the 200-foot-high staircase surely would.

5. **NOT DEMONSTRABLY EFFECTIVE**—Under OSHA, a prescribed safeguard must be demonstrably effective. Since an inch of foam would obviously not be effective to prevent serious injury from falling from a tower, the radio station cannot be required comply with the order.

6. **YES**—$300 certainly does not count as a being so expensive as to be unfeasible.

7. **NO**—The secretary's alleged change in the standard is ineffective. Section 6(a) only allowed the enactment of standards during the first two months of OSHA's life, from 1971 to 1973. Any changes to existing § 6(a) rules must be made according to the process of §§ 6(b) or 6(c).

8. **NO**—Under the Benzene Case, the secretary has the burden of proving that there is a "significant" risk of a material health impairment for which the standard is reasonably necessary. Proving that there is an "extremely minor" risk is not enough to justify the standard.

9. **NO**—A health standard is not economically feasible if it would force a large portion of an industry into bankruptcy, but bankrupting a few firms does not make the standard unfeasible.

10. **NO**—Remember, OSHA does not create a private right of action. OSHA does prohibit employers from taking retaliatory action against employees for complaining to OSHA, but OSHA itself must enforce this rule.

11. **NO**—To successfully assert the employee-misconduct defense, the employer must have established rules to prevent further violations and adequately communicated them to the workers. Under the circumstances, telling the daredevil Arto to spread the message was obviously inadequate.

IX. Workers' Compensation

1. **YES**—Unlike tort liability, there is no negligence requirement for workers' comp. As long as the injury occurred in the course of, and arising out of, employment, then workers' compensation is available.

2. **NO**—Workers' compensation regimes generally preclude tort suits by employees against their employer.

3. **PROBABLY NOT**—While states differ, so-called "mental-mental" injuries, where there is no accompanying physical cause or effect, are not usually compensable.

4. **PROBABLY**—A "mental-physical" injury such as this is compensable in most jurisdictions.

5. **PROBABLY**—If the employee was expected to be involved in the recreational activity, then the activity is covered by workers' comp. Here the employer was

heavily involved in the activity and got the benefit of improving employee camaraderie—both of these militate in favor of finding a reasonable expectancy of involvement.

6. **CATHLEEN'S, PROBABLY NOT; PAUL'S, PROBABLY**—In most jurisdictions, X-Radio could use the "aggressor defense," escaping liability for Cathleen's injury since he was an instigator of the horseplay. Since horseplay is otherwise usually covered by workers' comp, Paul's injury should be compensable.

7. **YES**—Although commuting generally is not covered, when coming back to work during off-duty hours, the transit time is usually covered by workers' comp.

8. **NO**—While injuries sustained during out-of-town work trips are usually covered, when the employee undertakes activities of a purely personal nature, workers' comp does not apply.

9a. **NO**—Since the drunk driver caused the accident, the employer's actions are too far removed from the collision to be a proximate cause.

9b. **NO**—Driving a car is not a risk that is peculiar to journalists.

9c. **YES**—Because Martha drives more in her job than most people do, her job presents an increased risk for injuries connected with driving.

9d. **YES**—Driving is a risk that actually accompanies Martha's job.

9e. **YES**—Martha was where she was because of her job, therefore the positional-risk doctrine is satisfied.

10. **PERMANENT PARTIAL DISABILITY**—Permanent partial disability compensation, such as for the loss of a limb, is often made according to a payment schedule, and not according to lost earnings capacity.

11. **YES**—Workers' comp preclusion of tort suits does not operate where the injury was the result of an intentional wrong. In some states, recklessness or wantonness will suffice.

12. **YES**—Traci is not at the Ziff Cafe in her employee capacity. Instead, she is a customer, and she can sue just as any other customer could.

X. UNEMPLOYMENT INSURANCE

1. **MAYBE**—Jurisdictions differ, but many states will disburse benefits if the employee had good cause for quitting, such as caring for a sick relative.

2. **YES**—Where an employee quits for good cause that is attributable to the employer, benefits are generally available. The atmosphere of sexual harassment here is attributable to the employer.

3. **PROBABLY NOT**—While the cases go different ways and different states set different standards, termination caused by the employee's own gross misconduct generally destroys eligibility for benefits.

4. **PROBABLY NOT**—Persons receiving benefits are expected to keep a personal appearance that would be expected of comparable employers. If long, unkempt hair is acceptable to rock bands in general, then Gerald's appearance is not a problem. If,

however, most comparable bands are like Third Blinking Goo Eye 20, then Gerald's benefits might be properly cancelled.

5. **NO**—Gerald only needs to accept offers of comparable employment. Working in FrugalMax is not comparable to being a musician in a rock band.

CHAPTER III

EMPLOYEE DUTIES AND OBLIGATIONS

CHAPTER IV

PRIVACY, EXPRESSION, AND AFFILIATION RIGHTS

CHAPTER V

DISCRIMINATION

A. Introduction

FOR BETTER UNDERSTANDING: basic terms and concepts

What is meant by "status"?

What is meant by a "class"?

What is a "model" or "theory" of discrimination?

Why discuss the models first?

B. Proving Discrimination: Legal Models and Theories

CHAPTER VI

WAGES AND HOURS

For the Equal Pay Act, please see Chapter V.E.

CHAPTER X

UNEMPLOYMENT INSURANCE